LINDEMANN GROUP
Peter Schiessl

CorelDRAW 2024

Training Book With Many Exercises

Also Suitable for CorelDRAW Essentials 2024 and Home and Student 2024

*Something looks different?
Use Window/Workspace/Default
(not by Essentials Edition)*

ISBN   979-8-304693-64-6
Print on Demand since Dec., 24th 2024
Translated into English (US) by Peter Schiessl
V241224 / LINDEMANN GROUP
Publisher: Lindemann BHIT, Munich
Postal address: LE/Schiessl, Fortnerstr. 8, 80933 Munich, Germany
© MSc. (UAS) Peter Schiessl, Munich, Germany
Contact: E-Mail: post@kamiprint.de / Telefax: 0049 (0)89 99 95 46 83
www.lindemann-beer.com / www.kamiprint.de

All rights prohibited.
Any use of pages or sentences of this book without written permission
of the author is a violation of international law and copyright.
Place of court is Munich.

This book is made with great accuracy, but neither author
nor publisher can take any liability for damages caused by mistakes
in this book or in the programs described in this book.
Alterations of content or price of this book reserved.

Some names and product names are registered trade names
of other companies. The usage of this book as a training manual
for the original product is not in conflict with
international trade names prohibitions.

This book was created from a full installation of CorelDraw 2024 in
November 2024. Deviations from the descriptions and illustrations
are possible due to a user-defined installation or changes due
to other installed software or as a result of updates.

Table of Contents

1. Principles — 7
- 1.1 The Corel-Family (Samples) 7
- 1.2 Workspace (not by Essentials) 8
- 1.3 Preliminary Considerations 8

2. Vector or Pixel? — 9
- 2.1 CorelDRAW or Photo-Paint 9
- 2.2 Vector-Graphics 9
- 2.3 Photos are Pixel-Graphics 10
- 2.4 By Comparison 11
- 2.5 Division of labor in practice 11
- 2.6 Essentials, Standard and Professional 12
- 2.7 The File Types 13
  - 2.7.1 Theory File Endings 13
  - 2.7.2 Show File Extensions 13
  - 2.7.3 Convert data types 13
  - 2.7.4 Example File Extensions 14
- 2.8 The Window "Learn" 15

TO DRAW *17*
with Rectangles, Ellipses, Lines, Colors *17*

3. First Steps — 19
- 3.1 Start Corel 19
- 3.2 The Drawing Functions at a Glance 20
  - 3.2.1 Selecting and Marking 20
  - 3.2.2 The Drawing Tools 20
- 3.3 Change, Move, Delete Rectangle 21
- 3.4 Rectangle Rotate or Distort 22
  - 3.4.1 Selection 22
- 3.5 Move and Copy 23
- 3.6 The Property Bar 24
- 3.7 Setting the Unit 24
- 3.8 To Save 25

4. Ellipses, Select, Colors — 27
- 4.1 The CorelDraw Construction 27
- 4.2 Set up the Page 28
- 4.3 Drawing Rectangles 29
- 4.4 Marking and Moving 29
- 4.5 Ellipses and Circles 29
- 4.6 Select Colors 30

5. Polygons and Properties — 31
- 5.1 Changing Line Thickness 31
- 5.2 First real drawing 32
- 5.3 Mark Several Objects: 33
- 5.4 Exercise "Move and resize" 33
- 5.5 Undo 34
- 5.6 Delete 34
- 5.7 The Color Palette 35
- 5.8 The Property Bar – Position 36

6. Zoom and View — 37
- 6.1 Zoom with the Zoom Tool 37
- 6.2 The Zoom Button 38

   6.3 Setting the Display 38
   6.4 Settings of CorelDraw 39
   6.5 Switch the Command Bars on or off 39

7. Lines — 41

   7.1 Freehand Tool 41
      7.1.1 Straight Lines 41
      7.1.2 Polygon 41
   7.2 Lines in an Angle 42
   7.3 Exercise Lines 42
   7.4 Exercise Convertible 42
   7.5 Pencil Types (not by Essentials) 43
   7.6 Paintbrush (not by Essentials) 43
      7.6.1 Artistic Media Tools 44
      7.6.2 Artistic Media Tools - Preset 44
      7.6.3 Artistic Media Tools - Brush 44
      7.6.4 Artistic Media Tools - Sprayer 45
      7.6.5 Artistic Media Tools - Calligraphic 45
   7.7 Smart Drawing (not by Essentials) 45
   7.8 Live Sketch (not by Essentials) 46
   7.9 Exercise Pen 46

PRECISE DRAWING *47*
Square, Circle, Grid, Guidelines, Text, Group 47

8. Precise Drawing — 49

   8.1 The Grid 49
      8.1.1 Exercise: Pyramids from Squares 50
      8.1.2 Further on the Grid 50
   8.2 Copy and Move 51
   8.3 Guidelines Setup 52
      8.3.1 Set Guidelines and Move 52
      8.3.2 The Guidelines-Menu 53
      8.3.3 Angled Guidelines-Menu 53
   8.4 Aligning On 54
   8.5 Exercise: Truck 54

9. Quadrates, Circles, Shapes — 55

   9.1 Quadrates and Circles 55
      9.1.1 Exercise: Quadrates and Circles with Guidelines and Grid 56
   9.2 Polygon, Spiral, Grinding 57
      9.2.1 Set-Up Polygons 57
   9.3 Common Shapes: Basic, Arrow, Flowchart etc. 58

10. Ruler, Zero Point, Group — 59

   10.1 Ruler and Zero Point 59
   10.2 Exercise: Railway Wheel 60
   10.3 The Menu "Transform" 61
   10.4 Group Objects 63
      10.4.1 Exercise: Blossom 63

11. Text and Symbols — 65

   11.1 Text Editing in Corel 65
      11.1.1 Text Formatting with the Property Bar 65
      11.1.2 Modify Text with the Pick Tool 66
   11.2 Exercise: Solar 67
   11.3 The Symbol Fonts 68

COLORS 69
Fillings, ClipArt, Photos 69

12. Single Fillings — 71
12.1 Overview select Filling and Adjust 71
12.2 Overview of Fillings 71
12.3 The Color Palette 72
12.4 Color Settings 73
12.5 Color Palettes 74
12.6 Smart Fill Tool 75

13. Fountain Fill — 77
13.1 Adjust the Fountain Fill 78
13.2 Multiple Color Filling 79
13.3 Exercise: Christmas Card 80
13.4 Exercise: Carton Home 82
13.5 Exercise: Steam Locomotive 83

14. Special Fillings — 85
14.1 Full Color Fillings 85
14.2 Bitmap-Pattern Fillings 86
14.3 Two-Color Filling 86
14.4 Texture Fill – the CorelDraw Fillings 86
14.5 Postscript Patterns 87
14.6 The tile size 88
14.7 Make a New Pattern Fill 88
14.8 Copy a Filling 88

15. ClipArt and Shadow — 89
15.1 Insert ClipArt or Photos 89
15.2 The Corel Assets 90
15.3 Exercise: Birthday Invitation 91
    15.3.1 Background for whole Page 92
    15.3.2 Shadow Tool (not by Essentials) 92
15.4 Insert ClipArt 94

16. Interactive Menus — 95
16.1 Interactive Fill Pattern 95
16.2 Interactive Mesh Fill (not by Essentials) 96
16.3 Interactive Transparency (not by Essentials) 97
16.4 Inserting Photos 98

SHAPE 99
Curve Editing, Text Options and Paragraph Text 99

17. Curve Editing — 101
17.1 Exercise: Party 101
17.2 The Stars – Move the Turn Points 102
17.3 The Moon - Circle Segments 103
17.4 Combine to Fill 104
17.5 Closing of the Figure 105
17.6 Add Turn Points for the Nose 106
17.7 The Figures – Adapt their Shape 107

18. The Snake – Curves Total — 109
18.1 First Preliminary Exercise 110
18.2 Second Preliminary Exercise 111
18.3 Serious Case: The Snake 112

18.4 The Head and the Points 113

19. Text Editing — 115
19.1 Producing Shadows 115
19.2 Insert Special Characters 117
19.3 Color Variety 117
19.4 Align Text to an Object..117
19.5 Add The Address 118
19.6 Other Adjustments for Text..118
19.7 Other Text Helps 120

20. The Paragraph Text — 121
20.1 Converting Text 121
20.2 Exercise: Business Card...122
20.3 Handling with the Paragraph Text Frames........................123
20.4 Print from CorelDraw 124

21. Pictures and Text — 125
21.1 Insert Photos 126
21.2 Cut Edge Areas of Photos..127
21.3 Insert Paragraph Text..127
21.4 Text Formatting and Hyphenation 128
21.5 Add a Page 128
21.6 Edit Photos...129

EFFECTS 131
for Text and Extrusion 131

22. Effects for Text — 133
22.1 Interactive Effects...133
22.2 Move Letters..134
22.3 Add Perspective 134
22.4 The Envelope Effect 135
22.5 Contour (not by Essentials) 136

23. Extrusion — 137
23.1 The Depth of the Extrusion..137
23.2 The Color 138
23.3 The Rotation 138
23.4 Light and Shadow 139
23.5 Bevels..139
23.6 Exclusion Exercise: Extrusion 140
23.7 Summary Shadows 140

24. Finally — 141
24.1 Overviews..141
   24.1.1 Basics 141
   24.1.2 Shortcuts 141
   24.1.3 The Drawing Functions at a Glance 142
24.2 A Title Sheet...143

25. Index — 145

Chapter 1

1. PRINCIPLES

In this book, we systematically describe CorelDRAW from the beginning and with many exercises. But to use this book and the powerful CorelDRAW program, you must have some prerequisites: general computer and Windows basics, e.g., experience drawing with mouse and keyboard, Windows basics: how to save files, open, rename, and copy files to a USB stick or to another folder.

That way, you will avoid frustrations and have much more fun with computers and this computer graphic course.

1.1 THE COREL-FAMILY (SAMPLES)

CorelDRAW is part of a package. Here a short presentation of the parts of this package.

The main content of CorelDRAW Suite:

- **CorelDRAW** is the vector-based program for graphics, design work, posters, presentations, business cards and more.
  - Most functions of Corel PHOTO-PAINT for photos are integrated into CorelDRAW so the switch to PHOTO-PAINT is mostly not necessary.
- **Corel PHOTO-PAINT** is for working with photos. Photos in the computer are created by scanning or taking with a digital photo camera, which are saved point for point (pixel = picture elements).

After the installation, you'll find on your desktop, these symbols:

The both main programs are:
CorelDRAW: the drawing program and Photo-Paint the photo program.

More Add-Ins: **Capture** (Create pictures from the screen) and the **Font Manager** (Manage fonts), **Duplexing Wizard** – depending on the version are not always included, not by the Essentials Edition.

More Add-Ins:

- **Corel Assets** (formerly CONNECT) is a utility that presents online clip art and photos from Corel, in addition to viewing or using Corel Cloud content.
  - ✎ With Corel 2024, Assets (Connect) is no longer a custom icon, it can only be started via Window/Dockers/Assets.

Using the "Launch" symbol, you can start installed apps and plug-ins or download more additional apps and plug-ins:

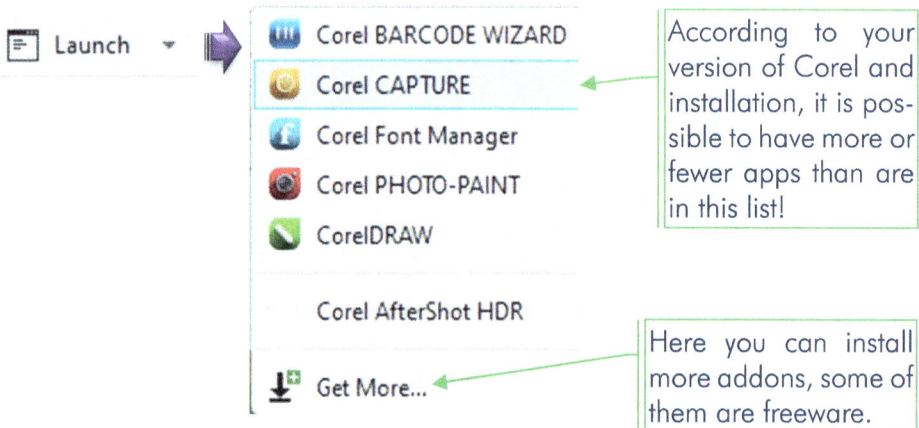

According to your version of Corel and installation, it is possible to have more or fewer apps than are in this list!

Here you can install more addons, some of them are freeware.

1.2 Workspace (not by Essentials)

When starting for the first time, a Welcome Screen appears there you can choose the workspace, Lite, Default or Touch or by Specialty Illustration, Page Layout and Adobe Illustrator:

- Depending on your choice, the icons and commands are arranged slightly differently.
- In the following we will use the working area "Default", the usual setting.
  - ✎ Lite is more reduced with as few symbols as possible, Touch is optimized for devices with touch-sensitive screens.

- You can choose the workspace in the welcome screen or anytime by the command Window/Workspace, we use by the following description "Default", that is the pre-set from Corel.

Looks different? Use Window/Workspace/Default (not by Essentials Edition)

1.3 Preliminary Considerations

A good cook cooks to the taste of his customers. Similarly, to decide if your graphic work is good, you must consider if it matches your customers' needs. So, think first about your target group.

Some suggestions:

- Advertisement for a music festival or business company?
- Birthday party for child turning 4 or 14 years old, or for a company event?

Generally, you can say that a younger customer enjoys more colorful and crazier designs. Today, many people have very good color laser printers, but they are not good enough for a professional advertisement.

2. Vector or Pixel?

CorelDRAW is a **vector drawing** program, while Corel PHOTO-PAINT stores the images as **pixel graphics**.

2.1 CorelDRAW or Photo-Paint

Why **CorelDRAW**, why **Corel Photo-Paint**? In practice, most times both programs are useful because they complete each other.

- **Photo-Paint** is for working with photos. Photos on the computer are so-called pixel-pictures because, simply, photos are created dot by dot, and the color of each dot is saved.
- **CorelDRAW** is used to make graphic works with prepared photos, text and clipart's such as presentation charts, promotion sheets or business cards/logos.

This working separation results from the big difference between both programs, similar to the difference between photos and drawings. This will be explained below.

2.2 Vector-Graphics

With vector graphics, drawn elements (lines, circles, rectangles …) are stored as mathematic functions (vectors): Line from point x1, y1 to x2, y2 with line width and line color.

For a line, therefore, the coordinate of the start and end point is noted, in addition to the line thickness, color and type.

- For this reason, each drawn element can be subsequently resized or moved.
- Even with an enormous magnification, the lines always remain sharp, in contrast to photographs and painted pictures.

In addition to CorelDRAW, there are numerous other vector-oriented programs, and therefore some different **file extensions** are used.

> Of course, all **CAD** programs are also vector programs (CAD = computer-aided design = computer-aided drawing, programs for technical drawing).

2.3 Photos are Pixel-Graphics

Similar to the screen, a picture is composed of many points. The color is stored for each of these dots (or pixels). Your screen might display the image with 1920 horizontal and 1080 vertical points (= Full HD resolution) - depending on the settings of your monitor.

This explains why image files become quite large and the following problem arises: small file - poor image quality or good picture quality - large file.

If pixel images of poor quality are increased, the dots are clearly visible. Instead of straight lines, stairs are recognizable as on old dot matrix printers.

Overview pixel-graphics

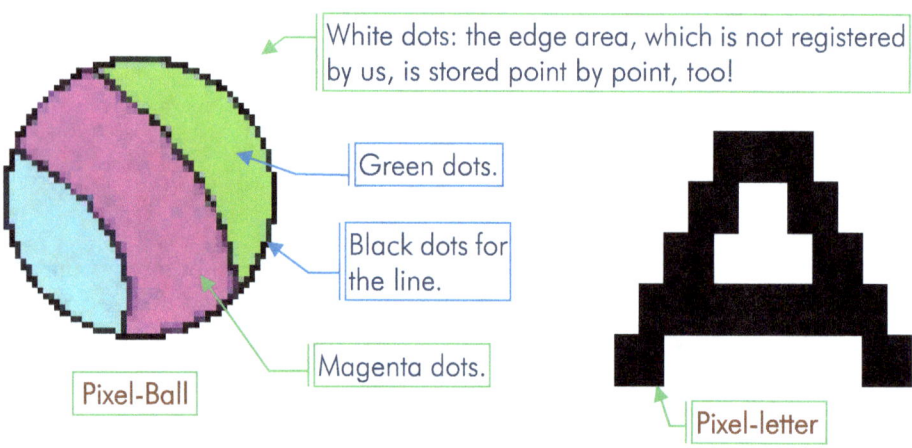

Compressing (Simplified explanation):

- When photos have large areas with small color differences, such as blue skies, high compression is possible:
  - Here, the compression function can be used to reduce the file size: instead of AAABBBBBCCCC, a formula can store this shorter as "3A5B4C".
  - In addition, other methods are employed, e.g., a reduction of the details and color differences and dividing into blocks that are 8x8 points each.
- Drawbacks:
  - Each time you load or save, the computer must calculate the compression.
  - A low-quality loss arises because the original image is slightly changed. This difference in quality, however, only occurs at higher compression rates above 20:1.

> The best compression comes from the .jpg file format, which has therefore become the standard format for photos.

jpg

2.4 By Comparison

The differences between the two formats explain the advantages and disadvantages.

Advantages of vector graphics (CorelDRAW):

- Small files with **sharp**, precise lines and edges.
- Objects (e.g., rectangle, circle) can be **changed** as desired.
- Special **effects** are possible, e.g., adding shadow to a text.

For that, still pixel graphics (Photo-Paint)?

- Pixel graphics are an unavoidable evil because a **scanner** scans line-by-line, dot-by-dot, saving the color of each dot.
  - Also, a **digital camera** stores the pixel by dot, e.g., from 18 million points per image.
  - Thus, **all digital photos are pixel images**.
- Another application case for a pixel program is **painting as with a brush** and color on a canvas. Many advertising graphics use this effect e.g., for pseudo-children's pictures.

Paint as with brush and paint on canvas

goes in Corel Photo-Paint: everything is painted over, which is why, as in nature, the previous state cannot always be restored.

> However, the border CorelDRAW to Corel Photo-Paint runs smoothly. **Detailed painting** to drawing, e.g., a wintery house with snow on the roof and smoky chimney, is already more useful in CorelDRAW because it can be corrected and changed at any time, and because e.g., a window is drawn only once, then copied as often as required, and Photo-Paint is to correct and prepare **photos** or copy an object out of a photo to use in a CorelDraw presentation.

2.5 Division of labor in practice

- First, prepare the pictures or photos in PHOTO-PAINT:
  - Scan or edit images (cut out objects, correct brightness, etc.)
- Then, complete the presentation in CorelDRAW:
  - Load images, add text and custom drawing elements.
- Consider **advertising**: there are photos (photo-paint) combined with other background and text (CorelDRAW).

For CorelDRAW	For PHOTO-PAINT (Pixel)
Presentations	Scan and edit images (for example, correct brightness, cut away edges).
Leaflets	Edit photos (for example, create an image section).
Title pages	Paint or modify images or clipart in pixel format.
Painting (detailed)	Painting like children.
Drawings	Cut objects from photos (e.g., a person. This object can be inserted into other files or photos).
Business cards etc.	

In PHOTO-PAINT, if possible, do not add text as text is converted into pixel patterns and cannot be changed afterwards. It is better to only edit pure photos in PHOTO-PAINT and add texts only in CorelDRAW.

CorelDRAW is not designed for text processing on a large scale. With a lot of text, work this way: prepare the pictures in Photo-Paint, the graphics elements in CorelDRAW, and import the results to a modern word processing program and assemble with text (layout).

If graphics elements are marked in Corel, they can be exported to the wmf- or emf-format, and then they can easily be inserted into all Microsoft programs.

2.6 Essentials, Standard and Professional

After the rapid drop in prices for software in recent years and the large number of even free programs, Corel has now followed suit and offers the inexpensive Essentials edition, a mid-range Standard version and the full-fledged Corel-DRAW Graphic Suite.

With these inexpensive editions you get an almost full-fledged CorelDraw graphics and photo paint program. Only a few functions that are really only of interest to professional users, such as program-supported perspective drawing or block shadows, as well as color separations and preprint functions, are reserved for the suite.

And the extras, many free clip art and high-resolution photos, are not included in the Essentials and Home and Student editions.

You can find an overview of Corel on the Internet at:

https://www.coreldraw.com/en/product/home-student/#compare

> This is why this book is suitable for all versions as an introduction to graphics editing.

2.7 The File Types

2.7.1 Theory File Endings

There are many different drawing and painting programs. Each of these programs uses a specific file extension. Why?

- The file name can be up to 255 characters from Windows 95 onwards. Even empty keys and customary characters may be used, but no "\" (backslash, because it is used to separate folders).
- The file extension usually consists of three or four letters separated by a dot from the file name.
  - In addition, a symbol for each data type and an explanatory text, e.g., "Data Type CorelDRAW Graphics" is shown in Windows.
  - The file extension indicates the program with which a file was created.

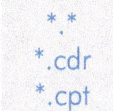

- As an illustration:
  - Filename.cdr (cdr as file extension for CorelDRAW).
  - Filename.cpt (cpt as file extension for Corel Photo-Paint).

2.7.2 Show File Extensions

So, it's handy to see the file extensions. Since Windows 95, the file extensions are unfortunately no longer displayed automatically. A brief guide for Windows 10 on how to do this:

- Start the Windows Explorer, click on the three dots "..." at the top of the command line, on the View tab in the list, deselect "Hide extensions for known file types":

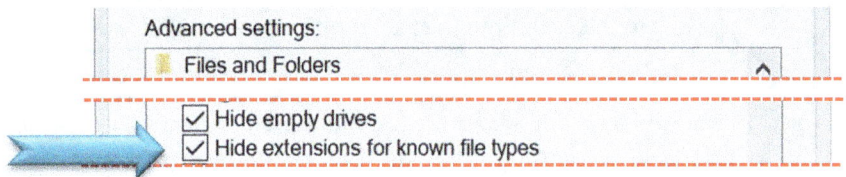

- As of Windows 11, it can also be found in the Windows Explorer directly under Ads/Show/File name extensions.

2.7.3 Convert data types

Usually, files can only be edited further in the source program. But not with good graphics programs. In Corel, almost every picture or graphics file can be imported.

- In the standard installation, not all import and export filters are loaded! Possibly. re-install. To do this, start the Corel Setup again and reload the desired file formats.
- ClipArt and vector files should never be opened in PHOTO-PAINT as this means a loss of quality due to the conversion to pixel format.

> PHOTO-PAINT only for photos (=Pixel pictures),
> CorelDRAW for vector graphics!

2.7.4 EXAMPLE FILE EXTENSIONS

A certain knowledge of the file endings is useful to recognize the file identities:

File extensions for vector graphics (drawings, graphics)	
cdr	CorelDRAW-drawing.
ai	Adobe Illustrator file
eps	Encapsulated Postscript: standard format for vector graphics (Originally Adobe printer language).
dwg	AutoCAD-drawing (abbreviation of drawing).
wmf	Windows Metafile: a format used by Microsoft, therefore, can be used in MS programs (e.g., Word) as well as emf (enhanced metafile).

The ClipArt elements from the CorelDRAW package are also stored in the cdr format, like the CorelDRAW drawings, and could therefore also be drawn.

File extensions for pixel graphics (photos, painted pictures)	
cpt	Corel Photo-Paint-picture
pcx	Previously, many ClipArt files were stored in this formerly widespread format.
bmp	Bitmap: Windows background images were saved earlier in this format. Today they are rare, since there was no compression!
tif	Target Image File: Formerly standard format for scanned images.
gif	Graphic Image File: Good compression, therefore recommended for pixel graphics, but max. 256 colors, not enough for photos.
png	Portable Network Graphic: With no-loss compression.
pcd	Kodak-Photo-CD-Pictures: Excellent picture quality, accordingly large files. When copying to the hard disk, the desired quality of the image can be reduced accordingly.
jpg	Very good compression, therefore very recommendable, especially for a very large image being copied to the cloud. Meanwhile, it is the standard format for digital photos. Also, most digital cameras save in this format, usually with very high compression.
Jp2	JPEG2000 was supposed to be the successor to jpg with improved compression and additional information, but it was not successful, jpg was simply too good and widespread.
jpg XL AVIF	Newer improved jpg formats with better compression and quality that would have a chance to replace jpg if they did not hinder each other (AVIF from Google vs. jpg XL).
raw	Without compression = without quality loss, used by professional photographers.

On the Internet, the transfer times are, or rather were, the problem, which is why pictures should be as small as possible: use jpg for photos going to the internet, and gif for drawn elements.

2.8 The Window "Learn"

A useful and helpful feature is the "Learn" window is displayed on the right. There you will find information and instructions on the currently selected tool and you can read more detailed help texts with the hyperlinks shown below.

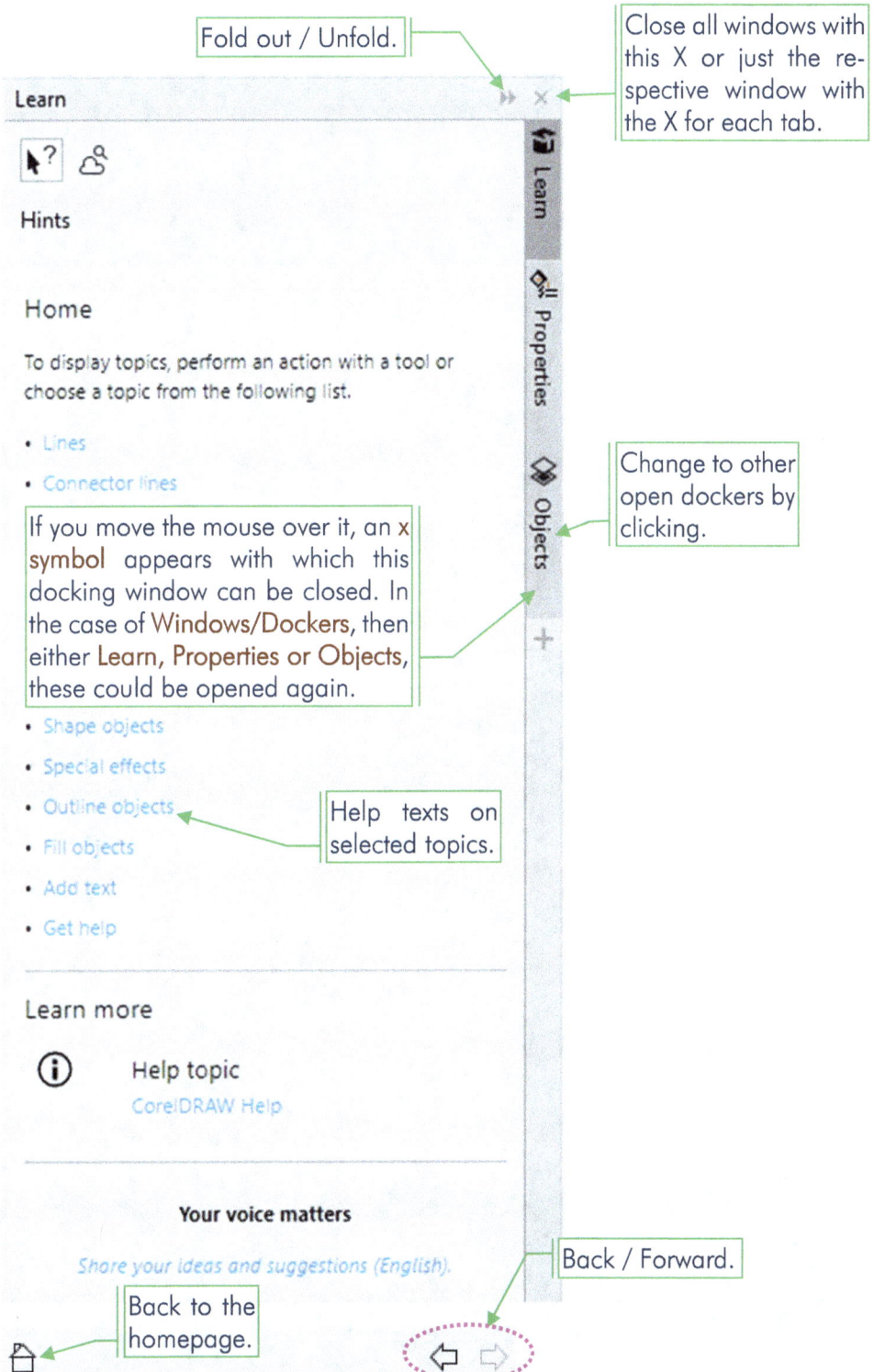

Exercises that you should perform are marked as follows in this book:

> ➢ **Close** all open docking windows (on the right in the Corel), we do not need them for the time being and can open them again at **Window/-Dockers/Learn** at any time.

First Part

TO DRAW

with Rectangles, Ellipses, Lines, Colors

Looks different?
Use Window/Workspace/Default
(not by Essentials Edition)

Chapter 3

3. First Steps

3.1 Start Corel

➢ Start CorelDRAW from the start icon on the desktop or in the Windows start menu by CorelDRAW:

CorelDRAW will greet you with this welcome screen:

"Get Started" to start a new graphic with one of this "+".

If you move the mouse over the "Welcome screen" the X symbol appears, which you can use to turn off this welcome window if you want to use the usual Windows icons shown below for new, open or save files:

Help/Welcome screen would be to turn it back on.

Workspace: not selectable with Essentials.

Most recently edited drawings will be displayed here later.

Here you will find e.g., some explanatory videos and Tutorials, on "Store" additional software, clip art collections and photos, currently, some of them for free.

Notice the symbols. Here you find the learning tools from Corel, e.g., some training videos.

Open an existing graphic.

Use one of the many Corel templates as a pre-set.

Let us begin the first drawing:

➢ Select a New Document in one of the ways described.

    ✎ Without the Welcome screen above, this is the same as in any other program with the icons at the top left (new / open).

➢ In the window that appears for the preselection, e.g., the drawing size, first switch to landscape format, then simply confirm with OK.

3.2 The Drawing Functions at a Glance

Before we start drawing step by step, we will first introduce **the most important drawing tools** of CorelDRAW in the tool palette on the left edge:

Important preliminary remark:

- If you place the mouse on a symbol for a short time, the **name** and a brief description of the function are reported. This is very convenient for orientation and searching for a suitable symbol.
- A **description** of the currently selected function is displayed in the Learn/Note window on the right side.

3.2.1 Selecting and Marking

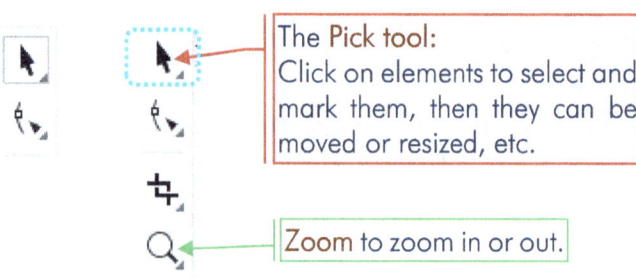

Note:

- If you want to **draw** something, first select the appropriate function (rectangle, line, etc.)!!
- If you want to **change** or adjust something, first select the desired object using **Pick Tool**.
  - Beginners often forget to switch to the **pick tool** and therefore draw many new mini-objects.
  - If you have drawn something inadvertently, **undo** it immediately, or **delete** it with the [Delete] key.

Accidentally drawn miniature objects complicate the selection of other objects and are often only recognizable as errors during printing!

3.2.2 The Drawing Tools

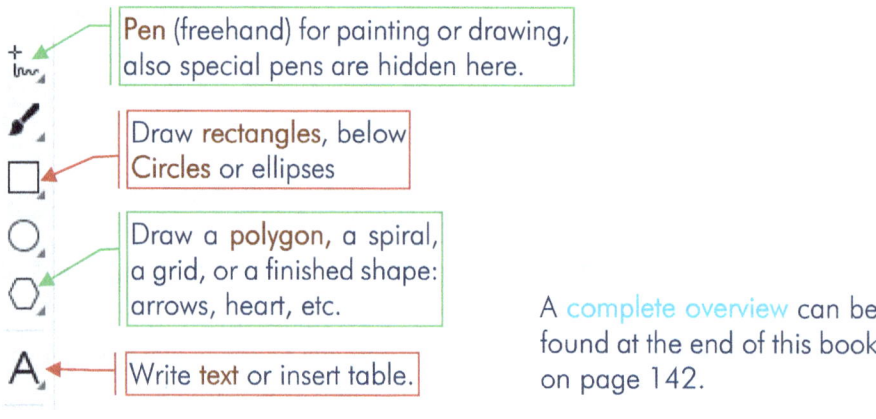

A **complete overview** can be found at the end of this book on page 142.

3.3 CHANGE, MOVE, DELETE RECTANGLE

Enough theory for the beginning, so that it doesn't become too much of it, let's start practically with our first drawing.

A rectangle is best suited to explaining many character functions most easily. After drawing, all elements must be pushed to the correct position and adjusted to the correct size.

Try it:

- ➢ Select Rectangle Tool, then draw a rectangle with the mouse button held.
- ➢ Immediately switch to the Pick Tool so that new rectangles are not inadvertently drawn.

The handle points appear. When the handles are visible, the rectangle is highlighted and you can position the rectangle or modify its size:

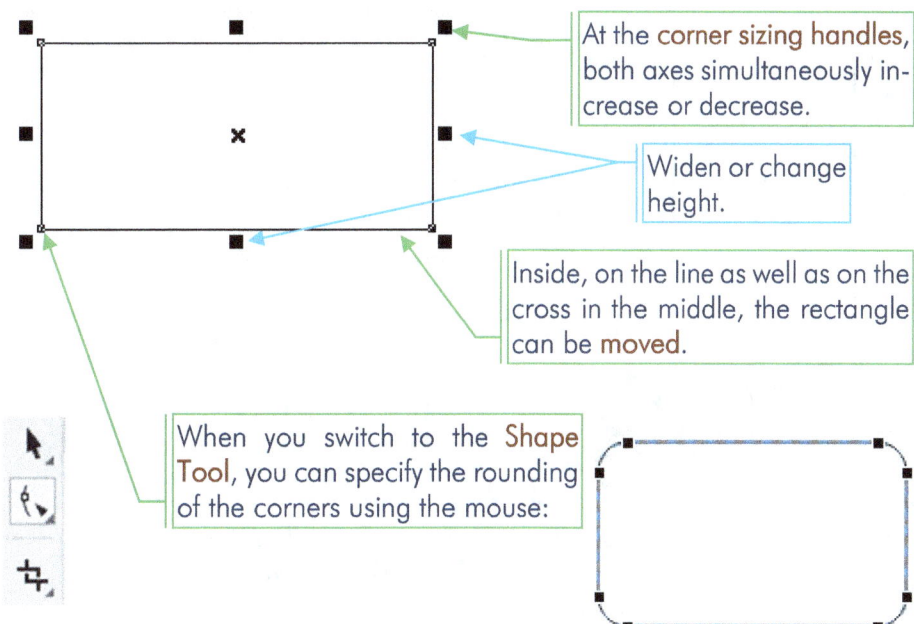

- ➢ Widen the rectangle to the right.
- ➢ Move the rectangle.
- ➢ Enlarge the rectangle on both axes at a corner sizing handle.
- ➢ Delete the rectangle: selected elements can be deleted with the [Delete] key.

To edit:

- ♦ Click the element so that the handle points appear.
  - ✎ You can change the size at the touch points, or
  - ✎ Click and hold on the item and move it, or
  - ✎ Delete the selected part with [Delete].

3.4 Rectangle Rotate or Distort

Corel provides other highly useful and very easy to use functions, e.g., to make a parallelogram from a rectangle, or to rotate it.

- Use the Pick Tool to select the object for the first time:
  - The grip points appear where the size can be changed.
- Click on the object again:
  - Arrows appear. With the arrows at the corners you can rotate, with those in the middle you can move parallel.
- Draw a new rectangle, switch to the Pick Tool and click on it, that the rotation arrows appear:

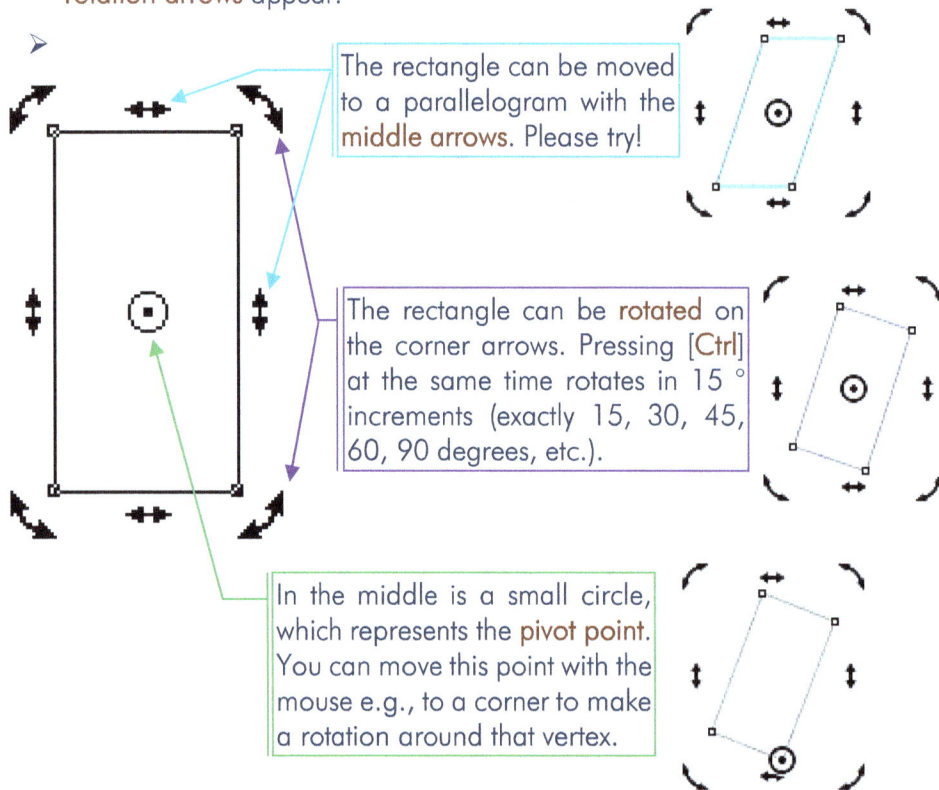

The rectangle can be moved to a parallelogram with the middle arrows. Please try!

The rectangle can be rotated on the corner arrows. Pressing [Ctrl] at the same time rotates in 15° increments (exactly 15, 30, 45, 60, 90 degrees, etc.).

In the middle is a small circle, which represents the pivot point. You can move this point with the mouse e.g., to a corner to make a rotation around that vertex.

- Try all options, draw new rectangles if necessary.
- Delete all rectangles.

3.4.1 Selection

Some symbols like the rectangle have a small triangle on the lower right. A selection menu can then be opened by holding down the left mouse button.

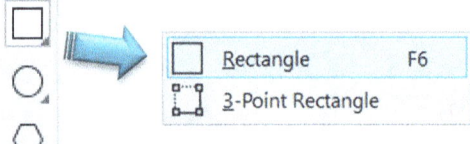

For the 3-point rectangle you do not have to specify three points, but with the mouse button pressed, draw the first line, then click once and draw the second line.

3.5 MOVE AND COPY

Drawings are labor-intensive. For example, with a wheel for a car artistically drawn, you will want to copy it and not redraw it.

Copying in Corel is very easy with a little trick:

➢ Draw a **rectangle** again.

Always use the Pick Tool:

- Always use the **Pick Tool**. Press and hold the left mouse button on the rectangle, and you can move the rectangle.
- Hold down the left mouse button, **move** the rectangle the same way,
  - but on the way **a short click on the right mouse button** and the rectangle is **copied**!
  - When you **press the left mouse button**, you have enough time to push the copied rectangle to the desired position.

copy

➢ Create the following objects by **copying** them with the right mouse button as described above.
  - If you hold down the [**Ctrl**] key, you can arrange the rectangles exactly horizontally or vertically.

Copying using the right mouse button is much easier than the normal way:

- **Select Object**, then **Edit/Copy**, the object is in memory, then **Edit/Paste** one or more copies or
- use the symbols:

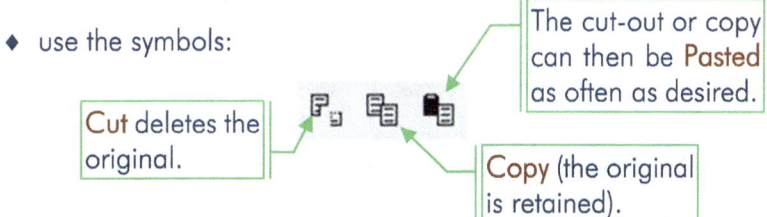

Cut deletes the original.

The cut-out or copy can then be **Pasted** as often as desired.

Copy (the original is retained).

The keyboard shortcuts are another option:

[Ctrl]-X, C, V
[Ctrl]-D

- [Ctrl]-X, C, V for cut, copy or paste.
  - C for **Copy** is easy to remember, the other buttons lie next to it. Otherwise, you can check the Edit Menu.

For making Duplicates you have some ways:

- With **[Ctrl]-D** or the Menu-Edit-**Duplicate** you get a copy.   **[Ctrl]-D**
    - ↳ You can modify the duplicate distance anytime in the **Property Bar** if nothing is marked:

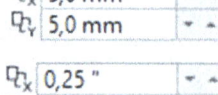

Finishing the exercise:

> Finally, as explained above, add a few rectangles by copying and pasting as well as **duplicating** and moving and rotating them.

> **Move and distort** the rectangles, even to form a parallelogram, for example try to arrange them similarly to those shown:

3.6 THE PROPERTY BAR

Note the **Property Bar**, which displays the most frequently required settings, depending on the selected object, for a rectangle, e.g., the position, the size, the rounding of the corners.

When you open the lock, you can set each corner individually.

You can change all values, e.g., the width from 2.276" to 2.3" and confirm with **Return** or a rounding with the arrows.

3.7 SETTING THE UNIT

> You can specify the unit, e.g., inches or mm, when opening a new drawing, in the property bar, unless nothing is selected, or under **Tools/Options/CorelDraw/Document/Page Size**.

In the Property Bar (see p. 28):   *By Extras/Options:*

Units: millimeters

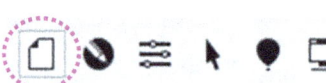

3.8 To Save

Our first exercise drawing should now be saved.

> Click on the symbol "Save" or use the shortcut.

[Ctrl]-S

We create a folder for our exercises. This goes directly in the File Save window by clicking "New Folder" (after you have chosen the left side the correct drive or folder in which you want to make a new folder, here "Documents"):

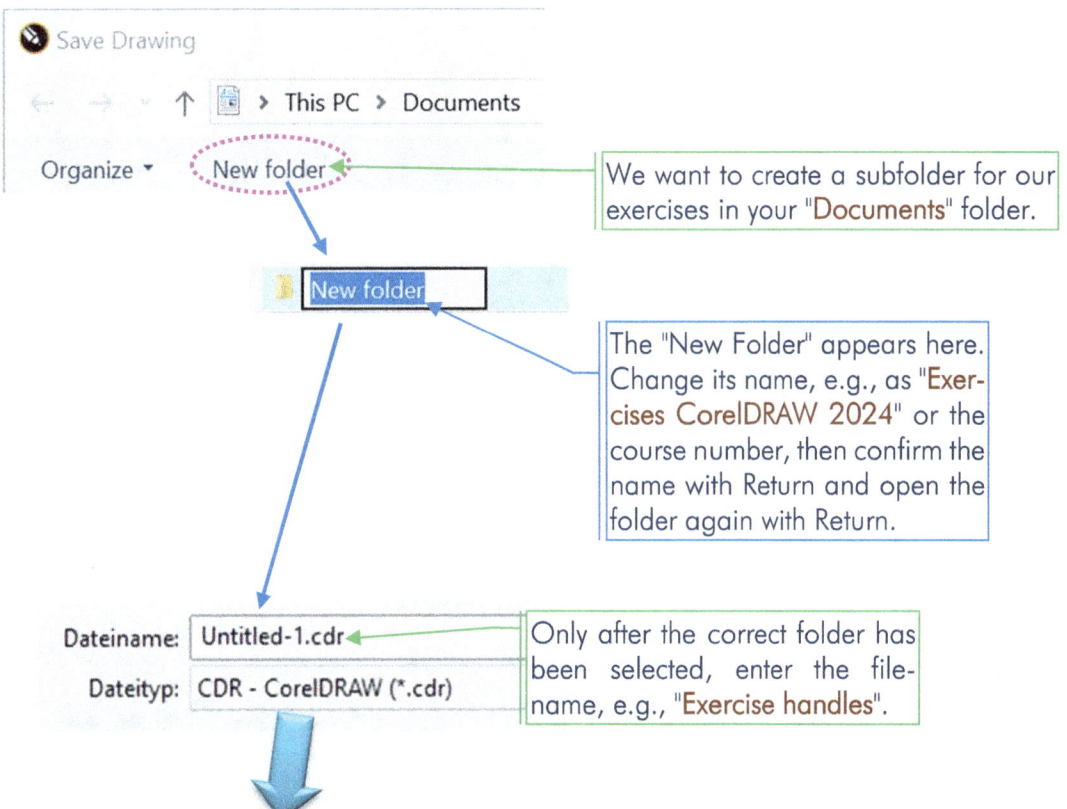

cdr from CorelDRAW

The file extension cdr is complemented by Corel. The file transmission is not displayed by default in Windows. Graphics professionals should change this as on page 13, because with the help of the file endings, it is very easy to identify which software or photo program a file comes from.

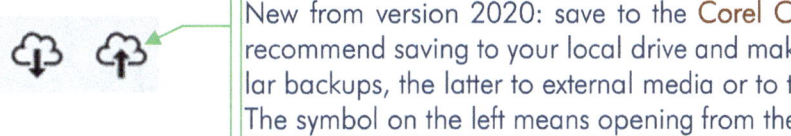

New from version 2020: save to the Corel Cloud. We recommend saving to your local drive and making regular backups, the latter to external media or to the cloud. The symbol on the left means opening from the cloud.

Before each save, check these two important settings:

1. Is the correct folder selected above?
2. Does the extension fit the file name?
   - If you do not enter a file extension or a dot, Corel automatically supplements the ending cdr, or leave the suffix right: filename.cdr

After saving, the new file name is displayed at the top of the Corel-DRAW bar.

Chapter 4

4. Ellipses, Select, Colors

4.1 The CorelDraw Construction

At the top is the command menu File ..., selected commands as icons in the toolbar, and the Properties bar. Notice: this is with workspace default.

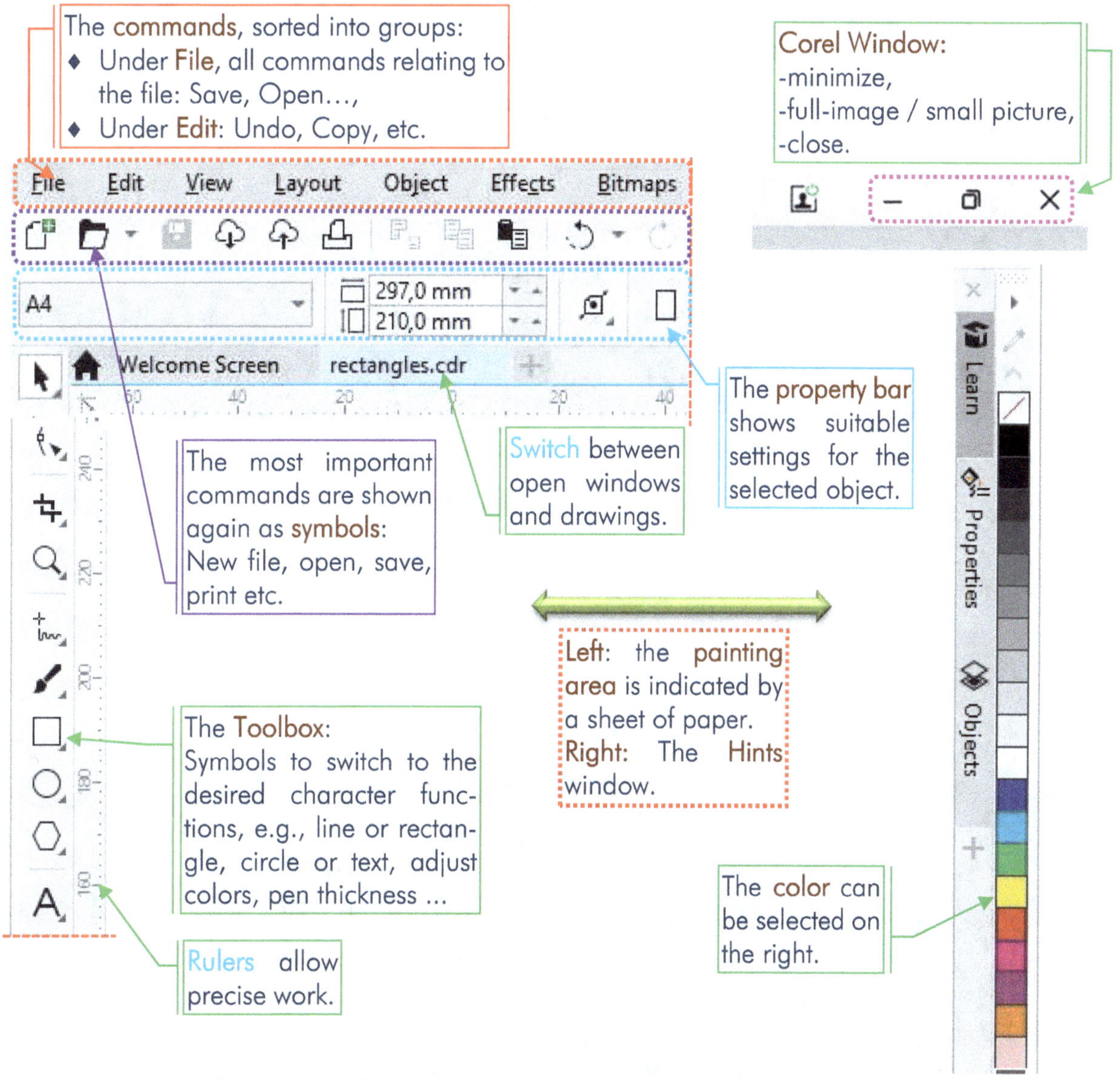

The commands, sorted into groups:
♦ Under File, all commands relating to the file: Save, Open…,
♦ Under Edit: Undo, Copy, etc.
Corel Window:
-minimize,
-full-image / small picture,
-close.
File Edit View Layout Object Effects Bitmaps
A4
297,0 mm
210,0 mm
Welcome Screen
rectangles.cdr
The property bar shows suitable settings for the selected object.
Switch between open windows and drawings.
The most important commands are shown again as symbols: New file, open, save, print etc.
Learn
Properties
Objects
Left: the painting area is indicated by a sheet of paper.
Right: The Hints window.
The Toolbox: Symbols to switch to the desired character functions, e.g., line or rectangle, circle or text, adjust colors, pen thickness …
The color can be selected on the right.
Rulers allow precise work.

➢ Close the Dockers Windows with the X, they consume too much space. You can turn them on again with Window/Dockers….

4.2 Set up the Page

For this new drawing, letter portrait format is not suitable. We therefore want to set the paper format to Half letter transversely. This will be in the dialog box, which appears after "new file" as well as at any time in the Property Bar (if nothing is marked). We recommend not using the dialog box to change the page format later in the drawing.

➢ Start a new drawing.

➢ Note: You could permanently switch off this window that appears when a new file is started, at the bottom left. ☐ Do not show this dialog again

✎ You can reactivate every time as follows: Tools/Options/CorelDraw, there activate "Show New Document".

➢ If nothing is selected, the page settings (paper size, etc.) are displayed in the property bar.

✎ Click with the pick tool in the empty area, so that nothing is marked.

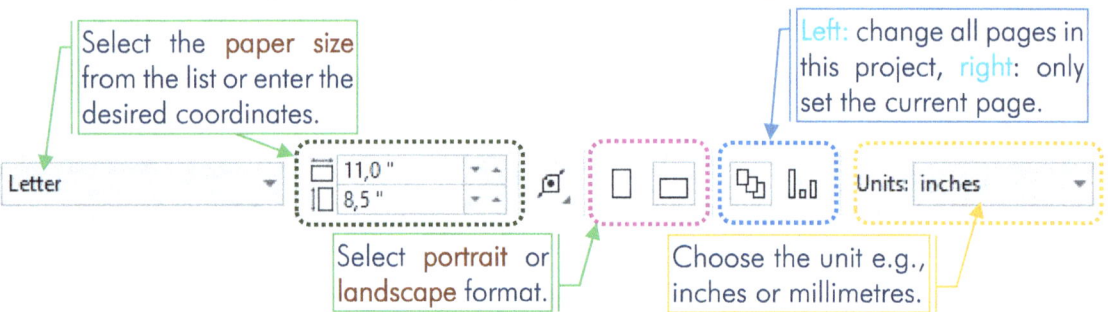

➢ You can also set the page size in the Layout tab. You should have a look at this menu.

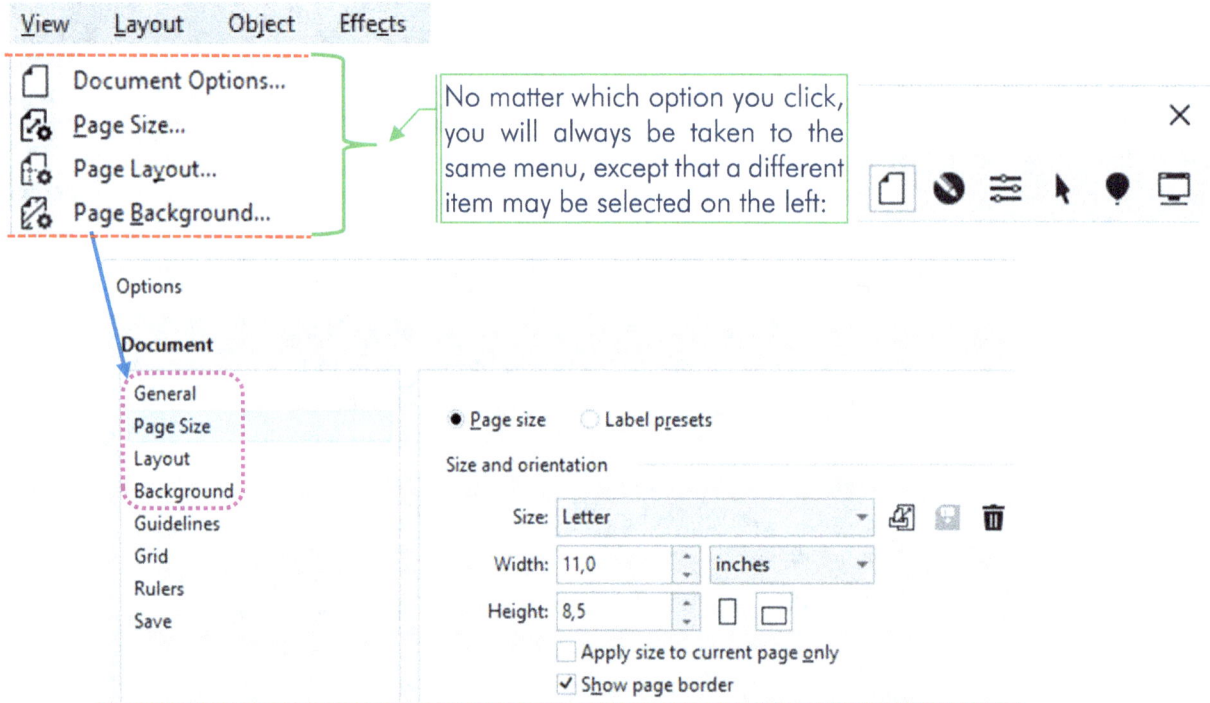

♦ For layout, you will also find the Page Background command: Select a color or an image (bitmaps, will be tiled if not the same size) as the page background.

4.3 Drawing Rectangles

➢ Now draw some rectangles.

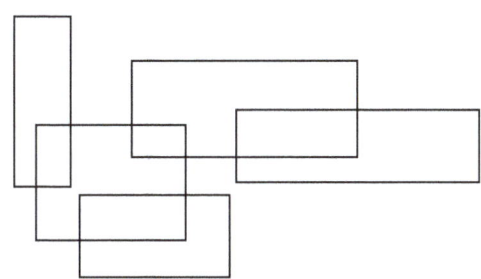

4.4 Marking and Moving

One object:

♦ Click on the Pick Tool to select it.

✎ The touch points appear so that the size can be changed, etc.

➢ Click on one rectangle at a time and move it on the page, then change the size of some rectangles and rotate them:

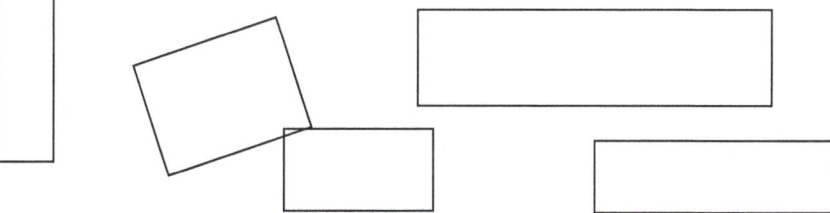

➢ Also hold down the [Ctrl] key and draw a square.

4.5 Ellipses and Circles

➢ And now draw some ellipses.

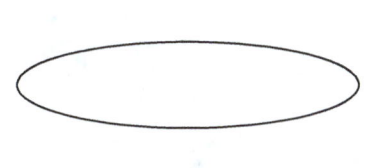
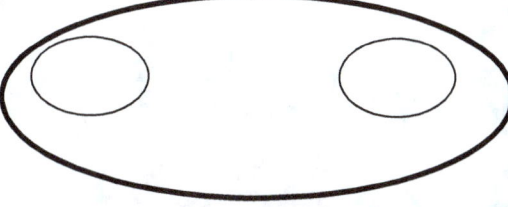

➢ Draw a few circles while holding down the [Ctrl] key

➢ Save as "Rectangles and Ellipses".

4.6 Select Colors

The rectangles are in simple black but somewhat bland. Let us make it colorful. Colors can be selected via the color palette at the right edge of the screen.

The following applies:

- First mark an object, e.g., a rectangle, then you can change the color of the selected object:
  - Click on a color in the color palette on the right edge. The following applies:
  - Left mouse button for the fill color, right mouse button for the line color.
- Change both the line and fill color for some rectangles, ellipses and circles.
  - Note: You can choose other colors at any time by simply clicking on the object in question and choosing other colors from the color palette.

First select the object or objects by clicking on them with the selection arrow.

With the left mouse button as fill color,
right-click the line color.

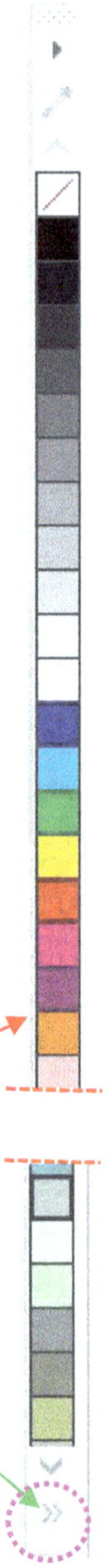

Herewith display the complete color palette.

It could be so colorful:

5. POLYGONS AND PROPERTIES

Without going into the depth of the diverse possibilities of this menu in these first drawing exercises, you can simply draw a few polygons, stars and shapes and color them.

➢ The shapes can be selected using the lowest symbol.

 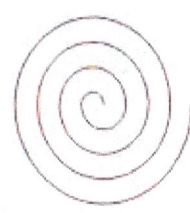 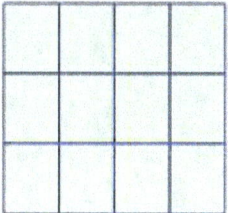

5.1 CHANGING LINE THICKNESS

In order for the outlines to become more visible, we can increase the line thickness for marked objects with the line icon in the Property Palette:

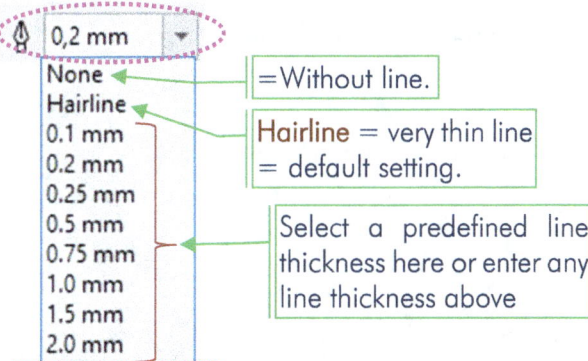

- ♦ All setting options can be found in the menu:
    - ↳ Window/Dockers/ Properties or
    - ↳ right mouse button/Properties or
    - ↳ [Alt]+Return if the object is selected.

> If the Properties menu is already open, even if it is collapsed, the above commands would close the menu, so first check on the right whether the Properties docking window is already open.

The Properties docker for a rectangle with line color red

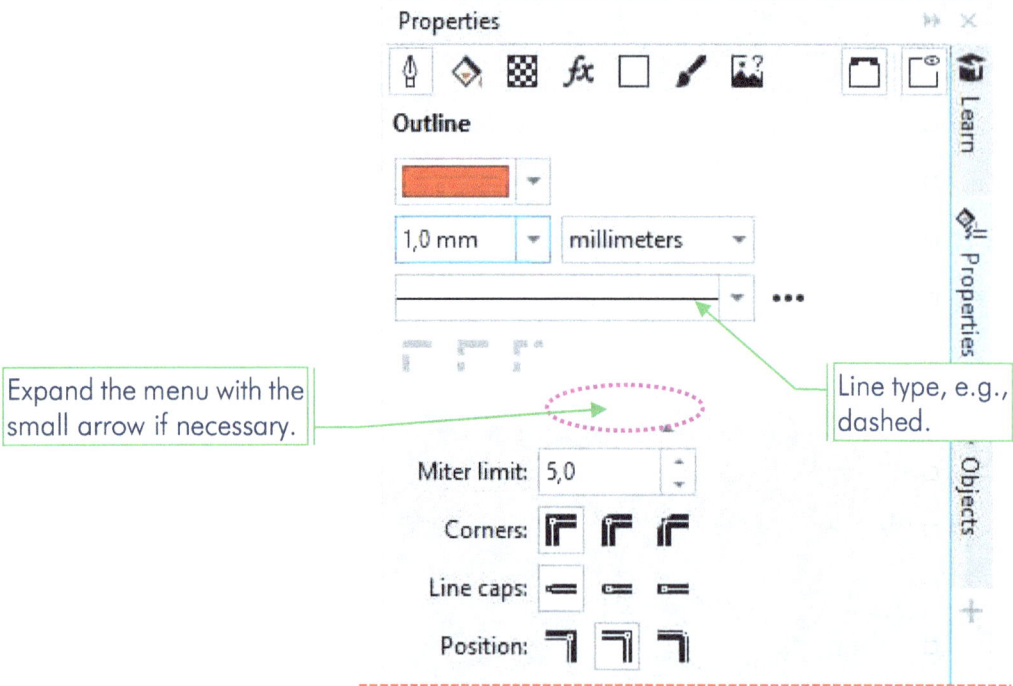

Practically:

- Use a large marking frame to select several objects and **change the line thickness**.
- Then, change the line and fill colors again.

5.2 First real drawing

You can now draw something with what you have already done.

- Another new drawing, this time **letter or DIN A5 landscape**.
- Try a similar railway carriage, simply made from **rectangles and circles**:

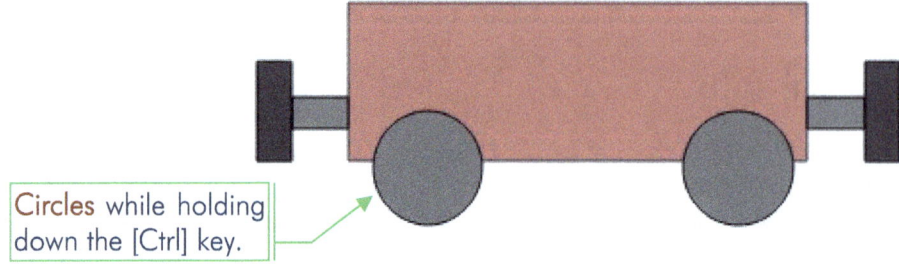

- **Save** as a railway carriage.

> You can see that this is still quite **difficult**, as we still lack tools for precise drawing (grid and guidelines) and quick copying, this will be covered in the next chapters.

5.3 Mark Several Objects:

- Can be clicked and selected by holding down the [Shift] key.
  - ↳ Note the message at the bottom of the status line: "X Objects selected...", otherwise it did not work.

Marking frame
- With the selection tool (pick tool) you can drag a large frame, just like a rectangle, except that the selection arrow is a marking frame.
  - ↳ All objects within this frame are highlighted and can now be moved, copied, deleted, and so on.

[Ctrl]-a
- Mark all: [Ctrl]-a or Edit/Select All/Objects (text, guidelines or nodes so marked, too).

5.4 Exercise "Move and resize"

Try this out on our train carriage practice drawing.

➢ Widen the page format fourfold to 600mm without changing the height.

➢ Select all drawn objects with [Ctrl]-a or a big marking frame,

➢ then move the first railway carriage, i.e., everything drawn so far, to the left at once, either

  - ↳ use the mouse to touch a line or
  - ↳ with the directional buttons, very precisely, or
  - ↳ specify the new coordinates in the property bar.

Exercise: Moving and Resize

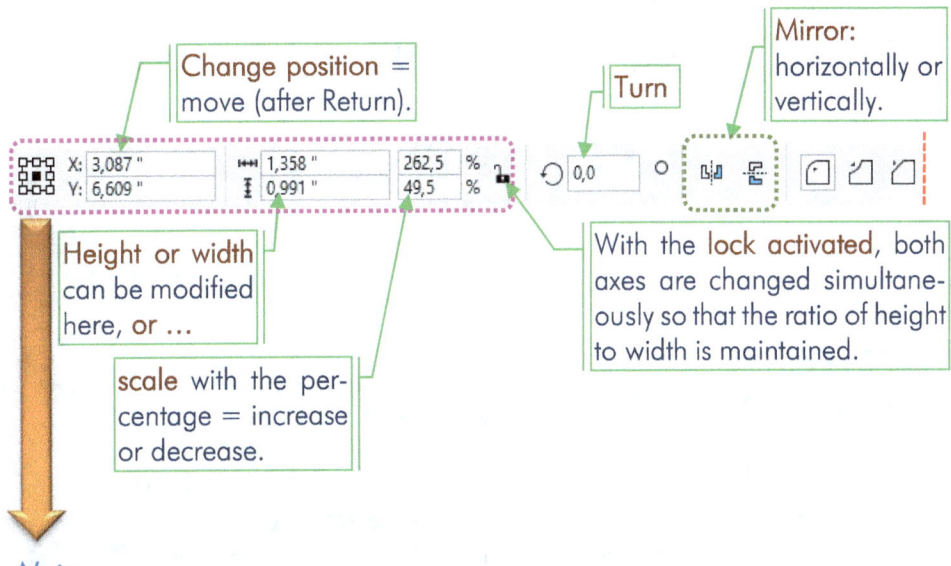

Note:

- The upper row changes the X-axis, or the width.
- The lower row changes the Y-axis or the height.

When moving with the mouse, make sure that all objects are still selected, because if you click next to them once, everything will be unselected. The group function, which we will introduce later, would help here.

> If the first railway carriage is moved to the left, copy and paste it.

- If all objects are no longer selected, select them all again. This is quite easy with [Ctrl]-a or a large selection frame, as we only have this one carriage.
- Move the copy behind the first carriage, making sure that the selection remains.

> Repeat the same until several carriages form a train.

> This was quite difficult, especially without the grouping tools, the drawing grid and the guidelines, which will be explained shortly. If something doesn't work, just undo and try again. That's why the undo command follows now.

5.5 Undo

♦ With the following advice, nothing bad can happen to your project:
- Observe the result on the screen for each action.
- If the expected has not been entered, select Undo immediately.
- Find the cause (wrong command, not marked, etc.) and find the correct command.

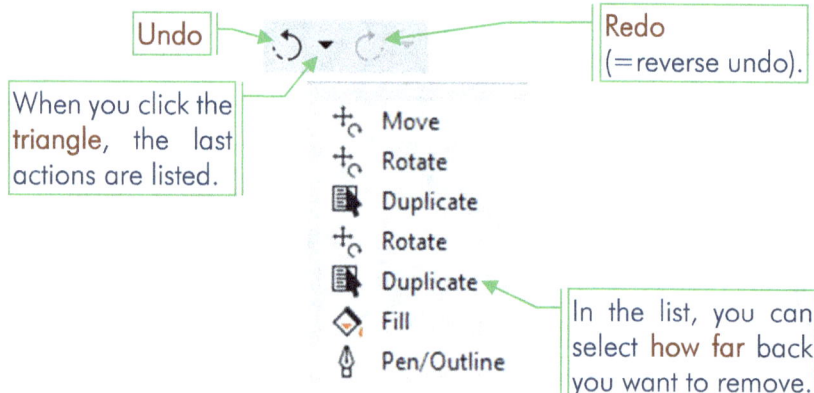

5.6 Delete

Of course, you can also simply delete objects that are not fitting:

> Click with the Pick Tool on the object to be deleted.
- Here, too, it is often convenient to select several elements with a selection frame or with the [Shift] key pressed.

> When the object is highlighted, which is recognizable by the appearing touch points, press the [Delete] key.

5.7 THE COLOR PALETTE

Only a few colors are displayed in the visible area of the color palette. The other colors are as follows:

Change to other pallets and various **commands**.

The / for turned off, means without filling or an invisible frame line.

From Black to **Grey** to White, then follows the other **colors**.

Turn On color palette

- If the color palette is turned off:
  - ✍ You can activate it again by **Window/Color Palettes**.
  - ✍ The default is the "**default palette**", we'll look at the other palettes below.

With the left mouse button as fill color, right-click the line color.

Attention! If nothing is selected, you will change the **defaults**. Cancel if warning window appears!

The color palette contains even **more colors**. Use these arrows to move the visible range or

herewith display the complete color palette.

➢ Assign a **line and fill color** to all drawn elements.

  ✍ In this case, too, you can select several elements with the [Shift] key or with a **marking frame** and assign a color to it at once.

At the **bottom left**, **colors already used** are displayed and can be assigned to other objects. At the **lower right**, the **fill and line color** of the active object is displayed:

Cyan, Magenta, Yellow, BlacK.

5.8 The Property Bar – Position

- In Corel, what was drawn last is front. If this is filled, everything underneath is hidden. If you have drawn the wheels last, they should be placed behind the car.

  - Instead of marking two wheels, it is easier to mark the car and move it forward.

➢ Right mouse button on the object, then Order:

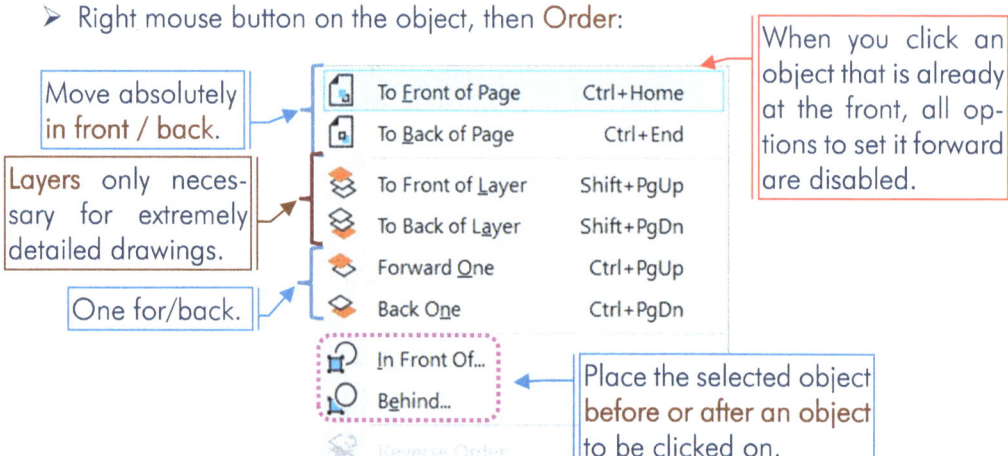

➢ You'll find it in the Menu Object/Order, too.

➢ Now select the polygon (if necessary, open this practice drawing again), set it to the front and set a different number of corners.

From Pentagon to Octagon:

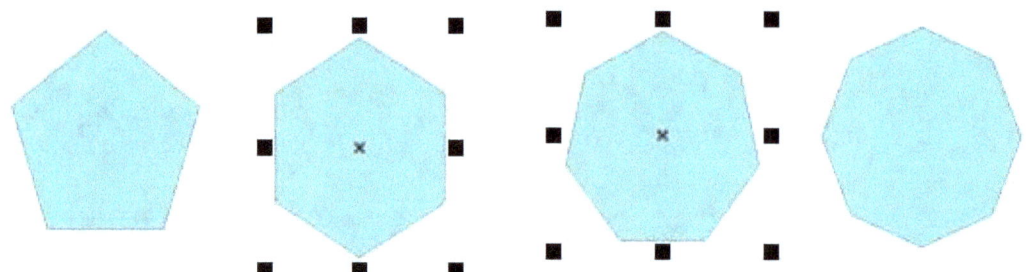

6. Zoom and View

If you expand your frame so that you can see the entire current drawing area well, many mistakes can be avoided from the outset, e.g., non-matching lines.

6.1 Zoom with the Zoom Tool

There are several ways to zoom. The simplest way is as follows:

- Choose the Zoom Tool on the left side.
  - You can now use the mouse to zoom:
    left mouse button = zoom in
    right mouse button = zoom out
    or draw a marking rectangle by holding down the mouse button.
  - Or use the icons in the property bar to zoom in or out (appears when the Zoom Tool is selected):

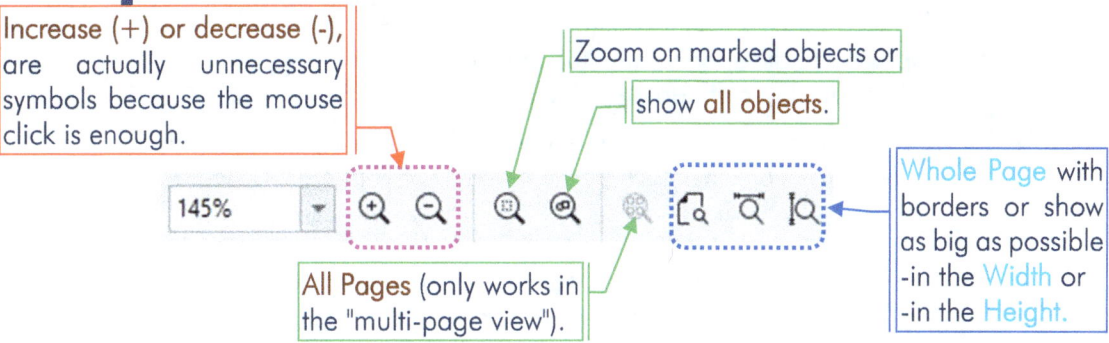

Increase (+) or decrease (-), are actually unnecessary symbols because the mouse click is enough.

Zoom on marked objects or show all objects.

All Pages (only works in the "multi-page view").

Whole Page with borders or show as big as possible -in the Width or -in the Height.

- With a Wheel Mouse you can scroll in/out with the mouse wheel also if the Zoom Tool is not selected and
  - the panning modus can start by clicking the wheel.

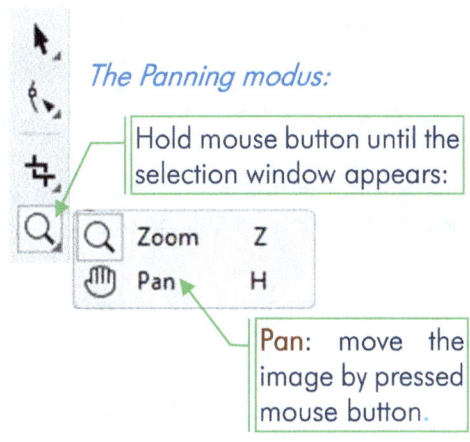

The Panning modus:

Hold mouse button until the selection window appears:

Pan: move the image by pressed mouse button.

Note the following Shortcuts:

- [F3] = zoom out,
- [F4] = zoom all objects,
- [F9] preview on whole screen, back with [Esc] or mouse click.

6.2 The Zoom Button

The Zoom button is also always in the Standard Bar:

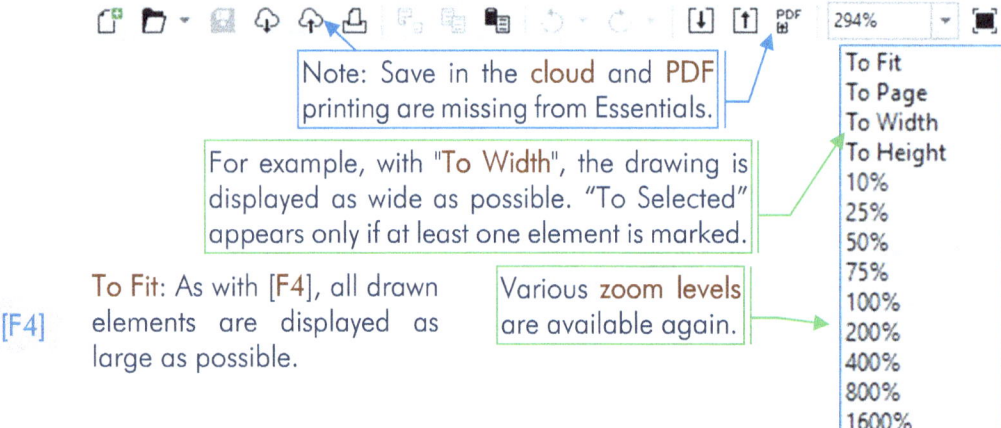

Note: Save in the cloud and PDF printing are missing from Essentials.

For example, with "To Width", the drawing is displayed as wide as possible. "To Selected" appears only if at least one element is marked.

[F4] To Fit: As with [F4], all drawn elements are displayed as large as possible.

Various zoom levels are available again.

6.3 Setting the Display

This information is presented here only because it can cause major problems, e.g., no fillings are displayed. In View, you can choose:

- For Wireframe, only outlines, but no fillings are displayed.
  - ↳ Previously this was sometimes useful to speed up the image build-up, nowadays in case of accidental switching, a dangerous option!
- Usually the display is Enhanced (postscript-fillings displayed detailed) or Normal (all, but postscript-fillings displayed shadowy).
- Pixels: with a higher zoom you see the pixels. But it is not as really printed. So, it uses only as much as the capacity of your graphics card.

Special view options:

- Simulate Overprints[1] – with Offset printing it is unfavorable if a bright object is printed over a dark one – this case can be displayed here.
- Rasterize Complex Effects: It can help by printing problems if complex effects are output like photos as pixel patterns.

In the View Menu, you will find these interesting functions:

- Multipage View[1]: Before printing once again, see all pages. To turn it off, select it again or press [Esc].
- Grid, Rulers, Guidelines: you can switch it on or off. Just try the grid for now, an explanation follows in the next chapter.
- Page: here you can e.g., make the "Printable Area" visible. This means the area where your printer can print is, most of the time, a little smaller than the page.
  - ↳ Page Border displays the set paper size so you can arrange the drawing elements appropriately (default is on).

---

[1] Missing from Essentials.

6.4 Settings of CorelDraw

- By **Tools/Options/CorelDraw** you can change the pre-sets of the Corel program,

- not by **Essentials**, by **Tools/Options/Customization** e.g., you can switch the Command Bars on or off, see next chapter.

- You don't really need the other menu item at this place, **Tools/Options/Global**, as you can switch to this menu at the top right: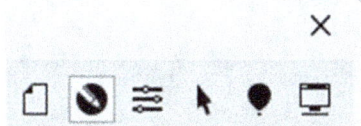

  - **Document**: start options for page format, grid, guidelines, background, etc.,
  - Settings relating to the program, such as the welcome screen, storage options, node settings in **CorelDraw**,
  - **Global**: here you will only find language, login options for user ID and background tasks.

- With **Tools/"Save Settings as Default"** you can save the current drawing settings as a general pre-set.

  - In the appearing menu you can select the desired options to be saved as pre-set.

  - This method also allows you to save the most commonly used paper size, as well as the grid and guideline settings, *as the default* for all new drawings.

6.5 Switch the Command Bars on or off

Not by **Essentials:** You can also turn on additional toolbars, for example, the Text Toolbar for font settings, or accidentally deactivated toolbars by **Tools/Options/Customization** by the point **Command Bars**.

Overview Command Bars:

- The **Menu Bar** contains File, Edit, View …

- The **Status Bar** shows additional information at the bottom of the Corel window.

- The **Standard Bar** is the most used bar at the top with New File, Open, Save, Print …

- Below is the **Property Bar** with most matching symbols, depending on what is selected.

- **Toolbox**: the command symbols on the left side with the drawing tools.

Exercise Command Bars:

- Turn on deactivated command bars, view them and turn them off again.
  - You can see the effect directly on the screen without having to leave the menu.

Move toolbars:

When working on graphics or photos,

it is sometimes helpful to drag a toolbar close to the drawing object in order to shorten the necessary mouse paths. By default, the toolbars are initially fixed and cannot be moved.

- The toolbars are initially fixed by default and cannot be moved.
  - This makes sense, because accidental movement can cause users a lot of problems.
  - But it is even better to learn how to move and move back and be able to handle it; this can save you having to move long distances with the mouse.
- You can enable this by deactivating "Lock toolbars" in the Tools/Options/Customization menu on the left, i.e., removing the check mark.
  - Also possible in this way: right-click on the toolbox or any toolbar (at the edge, not on a symbol), then "Lock toolbars" can also be switched on or off in the drop-down menu at the bottom.

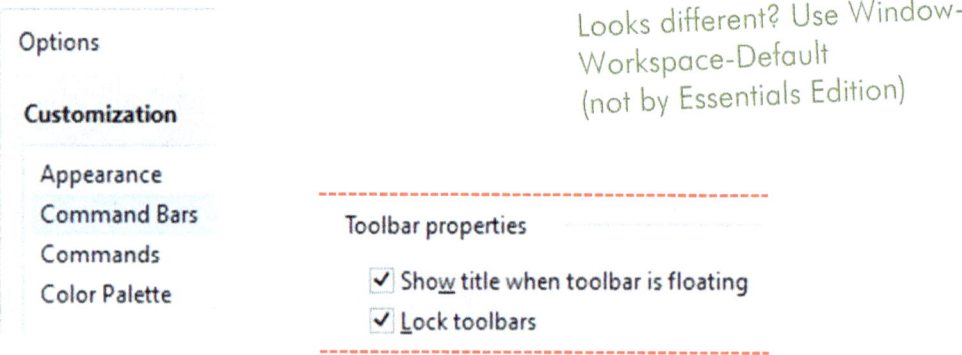

Looks different? Use Window-Workspace-Default (not by Essentials Edition)

Move toolbars exercise:

- Drag the Toolbox into the drawing and reshape the tool palette at the edges, as soon as the mouse changes to a double arrow.
- Close the Toolbox. Now turn on the Toolbox and push it to the old position (do not release the mouse too early).
  - Finally, click the right mouse button and choose Look Toolbars again.

7. LINES

7.1 FREEHAND TOOL

Lines are drawn with the Freehand Tool. There are several possibilities. We start with the freehand line.

➢ **Freehand Tool:** New drawing on DIN A4 transversely, then select the **Freehand Tool** and press the mouse button to draw:

➢ The lines are rounded automatically, fewer turning points facilitate subsequent shaping. More about curve processing on page 101.

> If you want to draw a lot of freehand, you should consider the purchase of a **drawing tablet** with a pressure-sensitive pencil, because the mouse is not suitable for freehand drawing. With such a pen the line becomes thicker when you press harder.

➢ Complete the drawing by switching to the **Pick Tool** and setting a different **color** (p. 35) as well as a thicker line (p. 31).

Not only freehand lines, even straight lines and polygons are possible.

7.1.1 STRAIGHT LINES

➢ For a **straight line** with the line tool:
  ↳ First mouse click = **starting point**,
  ↳ Click elsewhere = **end point**.

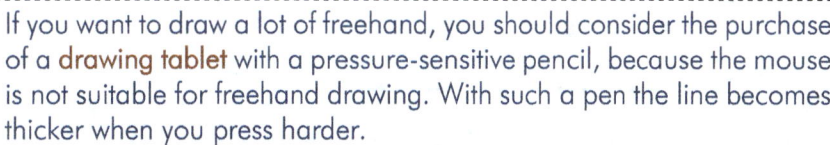

7.1.2 POLYGON

◆ The line tool can be used **to continue** a straight line:
  ↳ First mouse click = **starting point**, then move the mouse away.
  ↳ **Double-click** will set a point, but the line continues, so you can add with double-click as many lines as you want.
  ↳ Until you set the **end point** with one click.

➢ Draw a triangle or a carnival cap!

7.2 Lines in an Angle

Horizontal or vertical lines or lines at the following angles: 15°, 30°, 45°, 60°, 90° etc. can be drawn in this easy way:

- Set the start point as usual, move the mouse away, and hold down the [Ctrl] key.
  - If you rotate the mouse pointer around the starting point, you can see that the line is drawn only at these angles.
- Drag a horizontal line across the entire page:

7.3 Exercise Lines

- Draw the following in your drawing, then save as "lines and shapes":

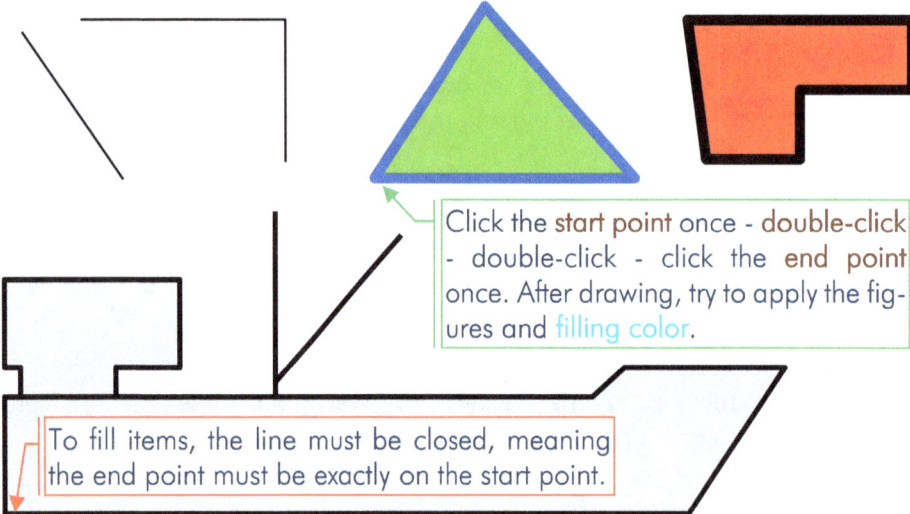

Click the start point once - double-click - double-click - click the end point once. After drawing, try to apply the figures and filling color.

To fill items, the line must be closed, meaning the end point must be exactly on the start point.

7.4 Exercise Convertible

- New drawing on letter or DIN A5 transversally and save as convertible.
- Draw a horizontal line as a road, draw a wheel as a circle (hold down the [Ctrl] key), set a thick line for the tire, and a matching fill color.
- Copy this circle when finished, for the second wheel, and also arrange it above the road line.
- Draw the chassis out of closed lines (double-click), then select a Fill Color and move backwards (right mouse button – order, or [Ctrl]-Page down) so that the wheels are in front. The symbols in the property bar disappear if more than one object is selected.
- Finally, draw the front disc as a triangle of lines, fill and set to the body of the car.

[Ctrl]-Page up/down

7.5 Pencil Types (not by Essentials)

Basically, this menu is very simple. In 99.5% of cases, you will only use the normal pen, the freehand line, or, depending on your taste, its complement, the polyline.

- The only difference is that the normal line continues drawing with a double click and ends with a single click, while with the polyline it is the other way round. It continues drawing automatically with a click and ends with a double click.

- The other line types are special cases that are therefore only used in special applications such as technical drawings or complex artistic graphics. For this reason, they will only be briefly introduced here, as this is not a book for professional users.

If you hold the mouse on the freehand pin tool, you can switch to additional line types in the menu that appears:

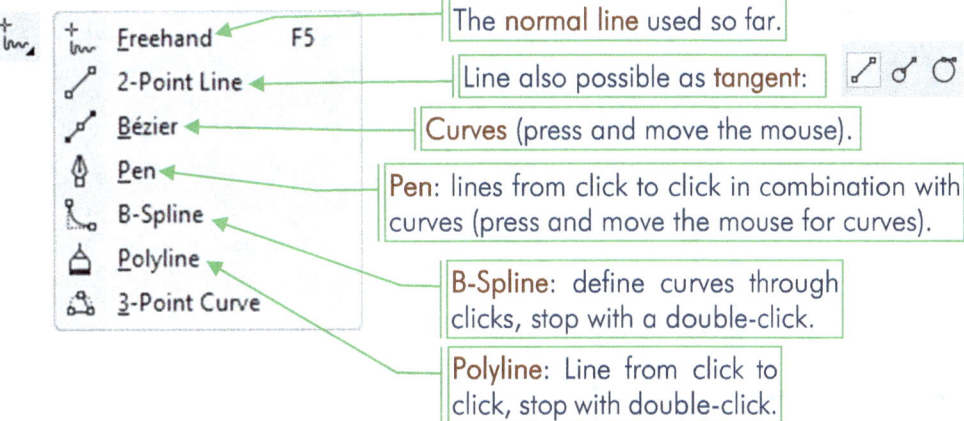

Instead, the "Bézier, B-Spline, 3-Point-Curve" curves are easier to create and adjust with curve processing. See details on page 101. So, in this menu only the Freehand line and the Polyline are recommended.

7.6 Paintbrush (not by Essentials)

Below the pen is the Artistic Media Tool with a variety of fascinating and interesting drawing features.

➢ New exercise and first choose the paintbrush, just start drawing.

➢ In the Property Bar you will now find the following setting options:

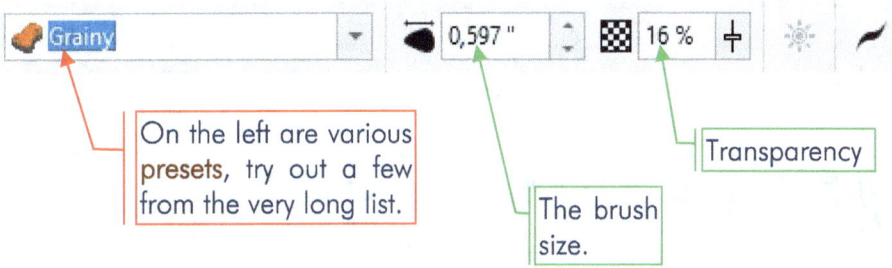

Please also note that the color (line color with the right mouse button) can be selected from the color palette on the right, even subsequently for selected brush strokes.

7.6.1 Artistic Media Tools

➢ Choose now the Artistic Media Tool.

➢ In the Property Bar you will now find the following setting options:

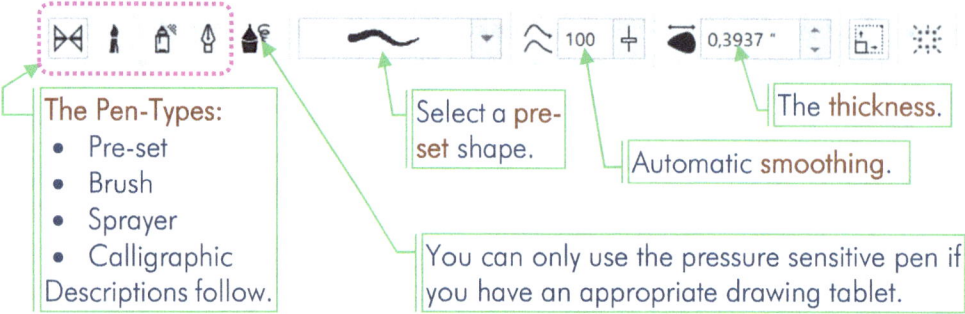

The Pen-Types:
- Pre-set
- Brush
- Sprayer
- Calligraphic

Descriptions follow.

Select a pre-set shape.

The thickness.

Automatic smoothing.

You can only use the pressure sensitive pen if you have an appropriate drawing tablet.

➢ On the left, select a pen type and shape for it, then paint.

♦ However, you can also change the shape after the object is selected or even assign the shapes to other drawn elements.

  ✎ For example, draw and mark a rectangle, then select a preset line shape or an image spray can.

  ✎ With Effects/Artistic Media, you will find these pen types again clearer as docking windows - please look through the long list to the bottom.

7.6.2 Artistic Media Tools - Preset

Instead of a line of uniform width, you can select specific line shapes, e.g., a wedge-shaped line or a water droplet.

7.6.3 Artistic Media Tools - Brush

These brushes paint beautiful wallpaper patterns on the page.

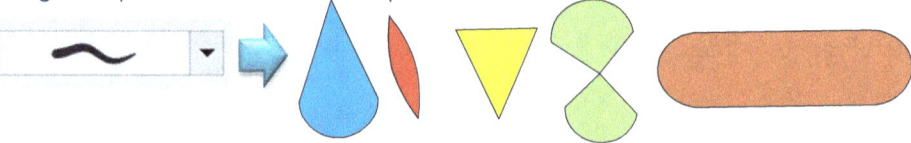

Note the type selection list.

First, choose left a type, then here a form.

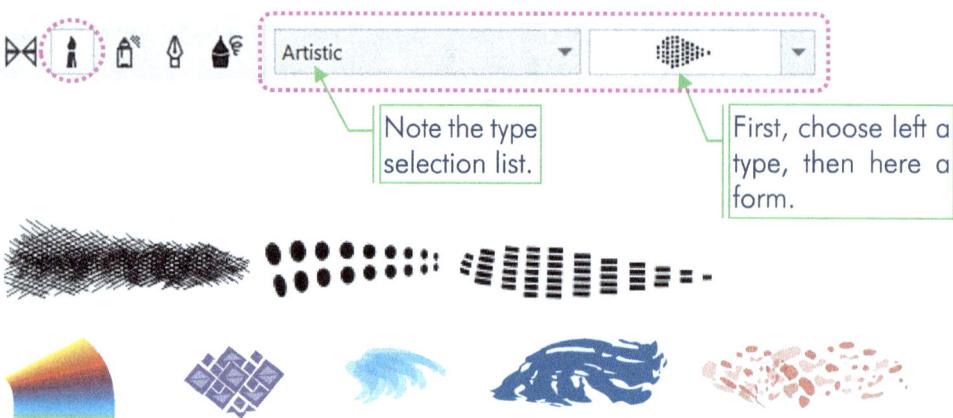

7.6.4 Artistic Media Tools - Sprayer

With the Sprayer you can **spray a series of images** with the mouse button pressed down. Try some types using the two selection buttons:

7.6.5 Artistic Media Tools - Calligraphic

If you paint sideways with a wide brush, the line is quite thin, but crosswise wide. This gives the calligraphic effects (e.g., when painting Chinese or Japanese characters). You can simulate such brush strokes with this function, whereby the width of the brush and the rotation can be specified.

- You can also find the calligraphy brush at **Painbrush/Artistic Media**.
- Draw a Japanese letter, first increase the angle for a flat brush to 60 °.

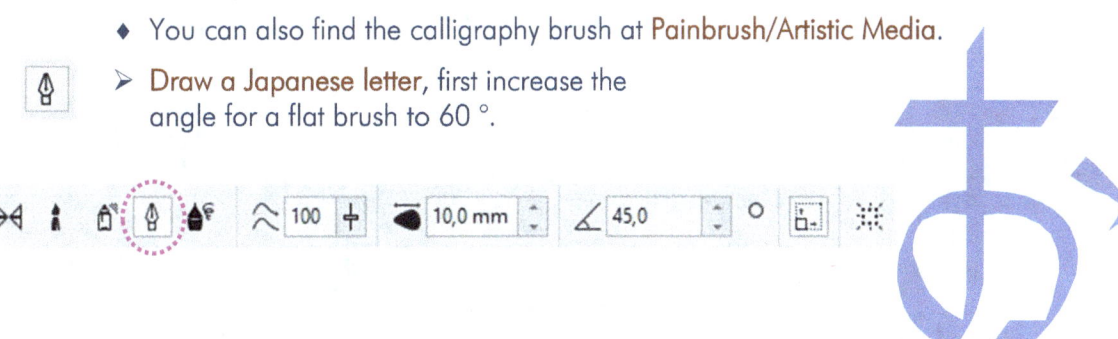

7.7 Smart Drawing (not by Essentials)

By the Artistic Media Tools, you can select the Smart Drawing Tool:

[Shift]-S

If the Smart Drawing Tool is activated, you can draw with a pressed left mouse button and Corel will try to complete and close a form (rectangle, circle, polygon…).

- Try it:

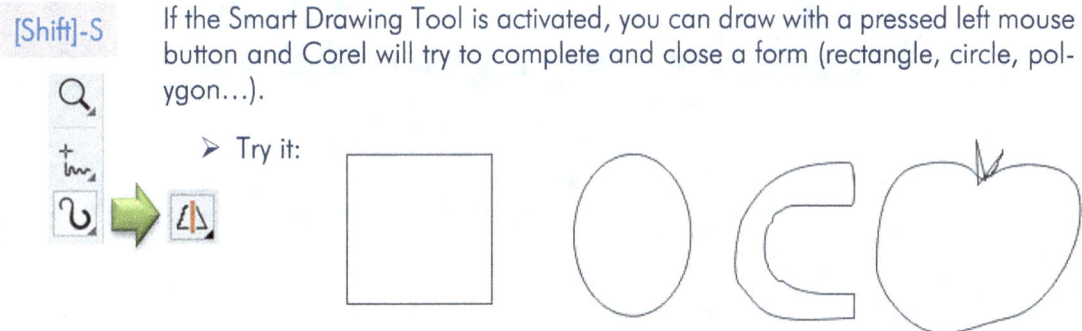

7.8 Live Sketch (not by Essentials)

This tool is a very smooth pen.

> Try drawing with it an apple or a car.

✍ Don't forget to close the molds, i.e., end point to the start point if the objects are to be filled.

7.9 Exercise Pen

> Paint with the **Pen Tool** the boat (straight lines), two rectangles for the blue sky and the darker water (fill blue), head and body as ellipses, and hair with the pen.

> The rest (clouds, balloons, waves, hair, ...) are brush or sprayer effects.

Sprayer for clouds and balloons.

Waves with the brush.

Try it and you see how easy it. is and realize your own ideas!

Two filled rectangles, light blue for the sky, dark blue for the water.

Notes: ....

....

....

Second Part

PRECISE DRAWING

Square, Circle, Grid, Guidelines, Text, Group

8. PRECISE DRAWING

8.1 THE GRID

The Grid is a useful aid in precise drawing.

- For example, if the Grid is activated, aligned, and set to a distance of 5 mm, all newly drawn parts are arranged on this 5 mm grid.
  - Crawling measures, such as a line from start point 45,05756 / 33,45666, are thus avoided from the outset and can be accurately drawn without any effort.

The grid can be set up most easy in this way: Right mouse button on the ruler, then "Grid Setup...":

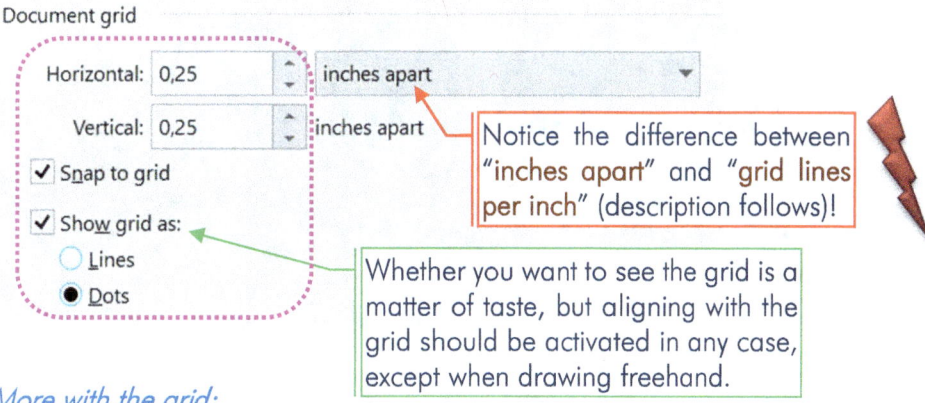

More with the grid:

- With View/Grid/Document Grid you can show or hide the grid points,
- With View/Snap to you can activate or deactivate the alignment of the various grids or guidelines.

  [Alt]-Y

  - Baseline Grid: Horizontal help lines similar to lined paper are displayed, their spacing can also be set in the menu above.
  - Guidelines: Sometimes, it is not enough to draw help lines into the drawing. Only when by View activated "Snap to guidelines", new drawings aligned with help lines.

Notes on the grid:

- 4 grid lines per inch = grid points every 0.25 inches,
  10 grid lines per inch = grid points every 0.1 inches.
- The grid points are automatically displayed with some space between.
  - If the view is very reduced, Corel removes grid points, so that a black drawing full of grid points is not displayed.

8.1.1 Exercise: Pyramids from Squares

Draw the following pyramid from squares.

- ➢ New drawing, Half Letter crosswise, adjust the grid to a distance of 0.2 inch.
- ➢ Then draw a **square** (hold down [Ctrl] key or use the grid) and **copy** multiple times using the mouse: [Ctrl]
  - ✎ **Move** and click the **right mouse button** on the way, and release the left button at the destination.
- ♦ When drawing, moving, and reshaping, note whether the cursor jumps to the grid points (if necessary, touch the corner).
  - ✎ If not, check to see if the grid is activated, the distance is correct, and the Alignment is set to On.

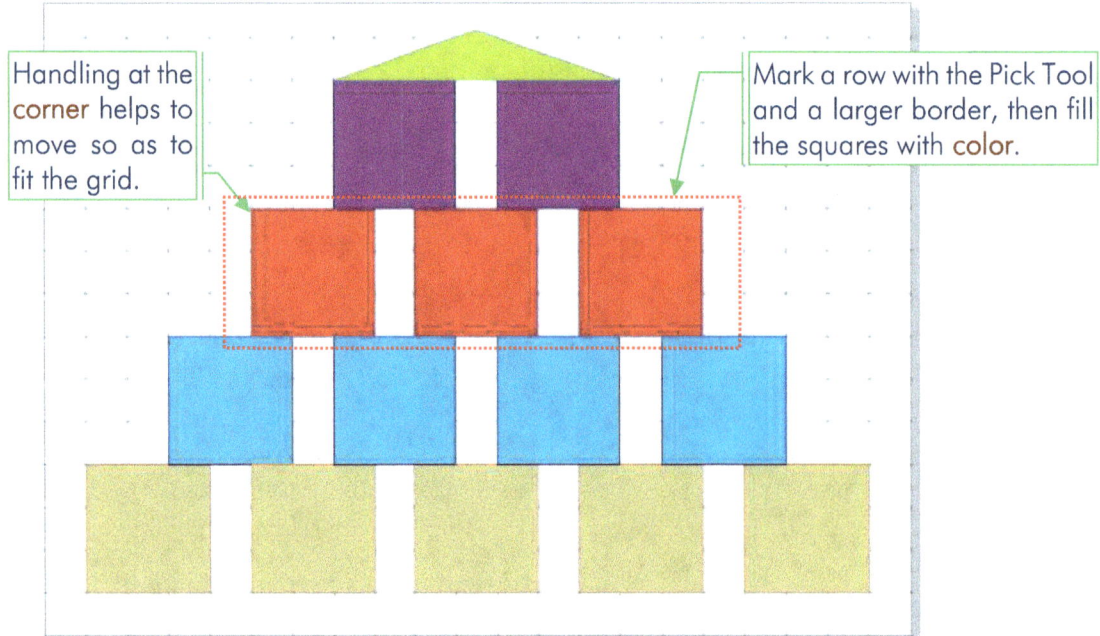

Handling at the **corner** helps to move so as to fit the grid.

Mark a row with the Pick Tool and a larger border, then fill the squares with **color**.

> While holding down the [Ctrl] key, you can draw squares instead of rectangles, circles instead of ellipses, and lines at these angles: 0°, 15°, 30°, 45°, 60°, 90°, etc.

- ➢ **Save** this exercise as "pyramid squares", as this is reused later.

8.1.2 Further on the Grid

Now we've set up the grid and can draw with it exactly. At least the good expression makes the change hardly noticeable.

- ♦ If you draw a **detail greatly enlarged**, you can fine-tune the grid, by every millimeter or even every 0.1 mm.
- ♦ The grid is optimal and should **always be used**, so that everything fits effortlessly. Exceptions are genuine freehand drawings, with [Alt]-Y, temporarily switch off the grid feature. [Alt]-Y

8.2 Copy and Move

- You can also create a copy using the Edit/Duplicate command.

[Ctrl]-D

☞ If no object is selected (if necessary, click with the Pick Tool in an empty area), the step size for moving with the direction keys and duplicate distance can be set there:

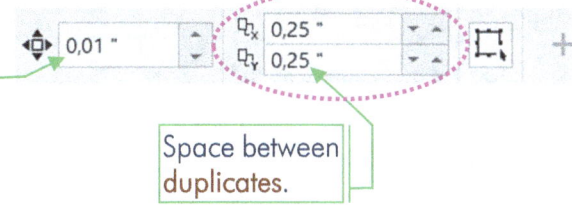

The step width when moving with the directional buttons can be adjusted at any time. Practical for precise and easy moving.

Space between duplicates.

The default setting:

➢ You can specify the step size in the property bar, or in the menu with double click on the ruler.

☞ For example, at 0.01", you can move the elements marked with the direction buttons by 0.01" each. The larger step size applies when the [Shift] key is pressed, e.g., you could specify 10 for 10x0.01" here.

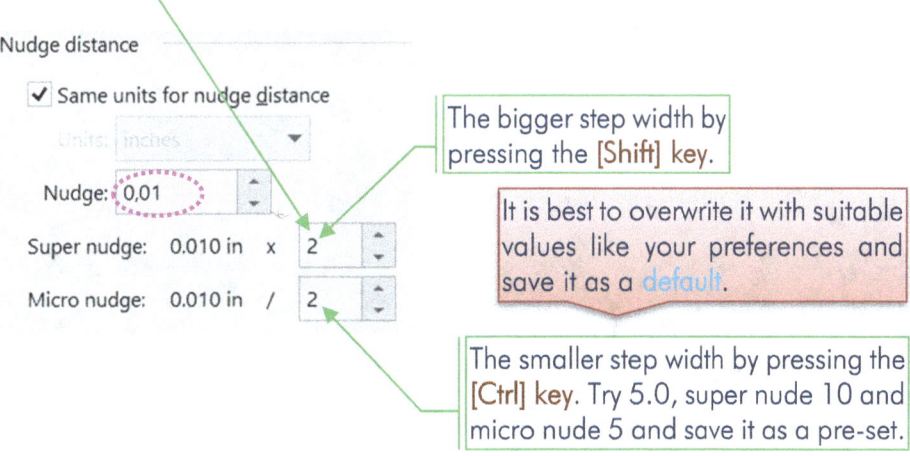

The bigger step width by pressing the [Shift] key.

It is best to overwrite it with suitable values like your preferences and save it as a default.

The smaller step width by pressing the [Ctrl] key. Try 5.0, super nude 10 and micro nude 5 and save it as a pre-set.

Exercise:

➢ Create rectangles and lines using copy, then rotate and move them to make the following farm. Make the work easier by increasing as much as you draw.

Draw once, copy often.

8.3 Guidelines Setup

The question remains: how are objects easier to arrange at the same height, e.g., the windows of the previous exercise? With the guidelines.

Important notes about the guidelines:

- Guidelines are not printed, but the objects can be aligned exactly on these lines. Guidelines are therefore optimal to specify page margins or to arrange elements flush.
- Rulers/Grid/Guidelines visible/invisible and adjust the alignment:

8.3.1 Set Guidelines and Move

The rulers are located at the top and left from the drawing area:

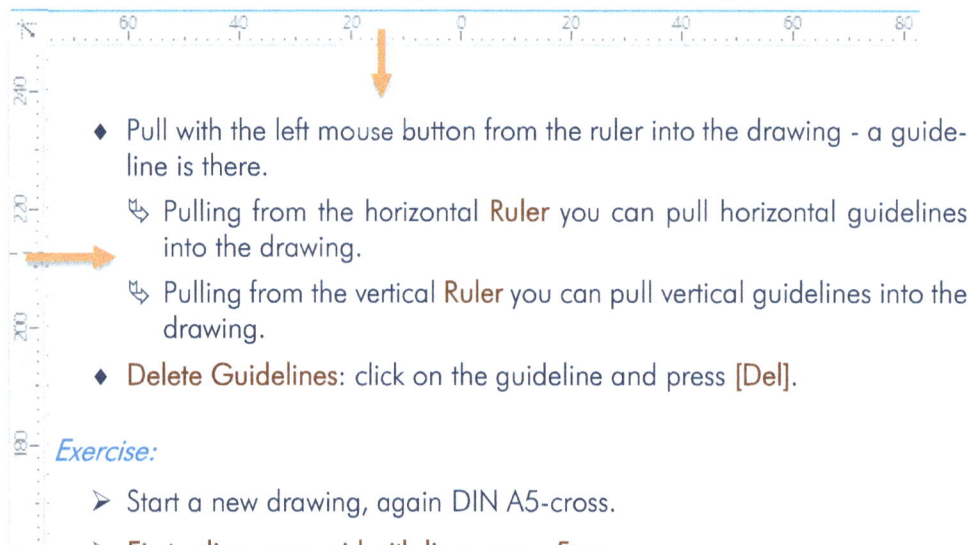

- Pull with the left mouse button from the ruler into the drawing - a guideline is there.
  - Pulling from the horizontal Ruler you can pull horizontal guidelines into the drawing.
  - Pulling from the vertical Ruler you can pull vertical guidelines into the drawing.
- Delete Guidelines: click on the guideline and press [Del].

Exercise:

- Start a new drawing, again DIN A5-cross.
- First, align your grid with lines every 5mm.
  - If you now draw guidelines into the drawing, they will also be aligned to the grid as long as you release the mouse near a grid point (note the appearing marks).
- Then drag two horizontal and two vertical guides as side-edges into the drawing.

Move Guidelines:

- Try to move a vertical and a horizontal help line: click and drag them to another location.

Now we turn a Guideline:

- Pull another guideline in the middle of it. When clicking on it, the arrows on which the guideline can be rotated appear outside.
  - You can also specify the angle of rotation in the property bar (confirm with Return). Right of the angle you can set the center of rotation.

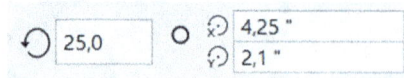

8.3.2 The Guidelines-Menu

♦ The guideline menu is useful when many help lines are set:
  ↳ To open the menu, double click on a guideline or
  ↳ Right mouse button on the Ruler, then "Guidelines Setup" or
  ↳ Tools/Options/CorelDraw, then switch to Document in the upper right corner and select the Guidelines item on the left.

Click on Guidelines on the left, then you can set the visibility on the first tab and activate alignment with the auxiliary lines.

In the guidelines menu you will find index cards for horizontal, vertical and all auxiliary lines, as well as default settings, here are various default settings such as for each 1cm margin.

Note that you can set new auxiliary lines as well as move existing ones on each tab, e.g., to move an auxiliary line from crooked coordinates to the nearest straight coordinates.

The menu Tools/Options/CorelDRAW/Document/Guidelines:

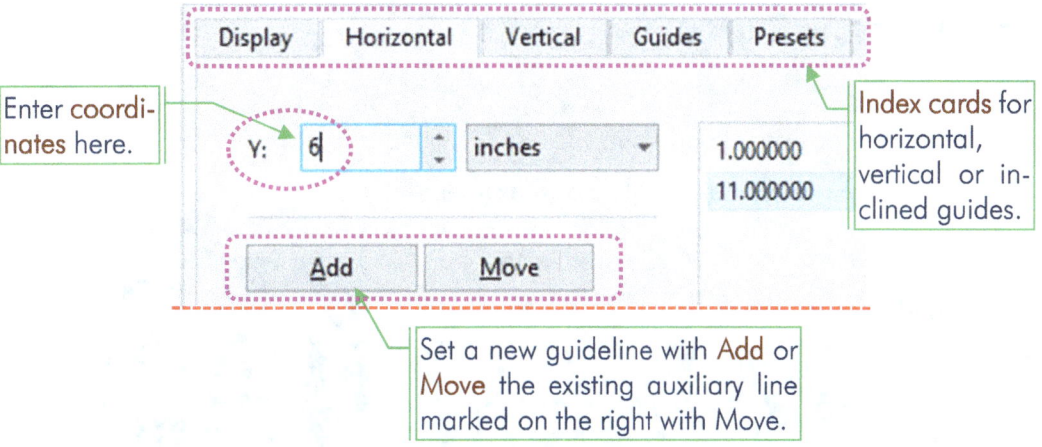

Snap to Guides can also be activated at the top of the toolbar:

8.3.3 Angled Guidelines-Menu

On the Guides tab, you can also specify an angle or change the angle for an existing auxiliary line. However, this would also be possible in the property bar when a guide is clicked:

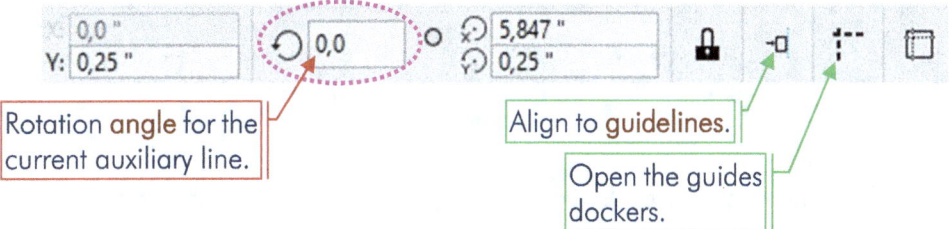

When you first set up the grid, guidelines are pulled into the drawing as desired.

8.4 Aligning On

The help lines are not used as long as the objects are not aligned with them. A number of settings can also be made in this regard in the View menu.

[Alt]-Y

- With **View** you can switch on/off the visibility of the Grid or Guidelines.
- With **View/Snap To** you can switch on/off the snap function of the Grid or Guidelines.
- **Dynamic guidelines** make constructing easier, since they appear automatically and indicate angles or references.
- Alignment switched off or [Alt] -Q switches all alignment variants (on auxiliary lines, grids, etc.) off or on again as previously set.

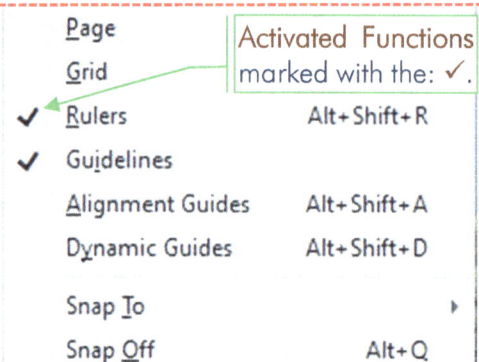

8.5 Exercise: Truck

- Start a new drawing crosswise and save as "Truck".
- Also possible: Page setup: 6 x 3 meters and grid each 0.2 m.
- Set below a horizontal line as the street.

So it should be:

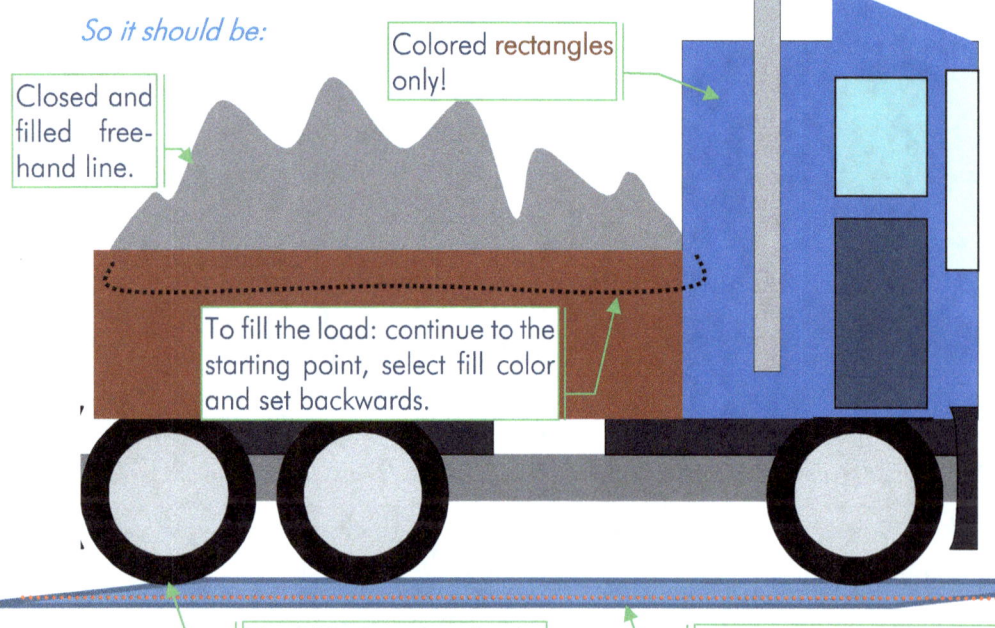

The Wheels:

- Draw the wheels as **circles** by pressing [Ctrl] or using the grid so it doesn't become an ellipse.
- Copy the first **wheel** twice. If you press [Shift] by copying you can move them exactly horizontally.

9. Quadrates, Circles, Shapes

9.1 Quadrates and Circles

We have already created squares and circles by pressing the [Ctrl] key in the truck exercise before.

- By pressing [Ctrl]-Left Mouse Button you can draw
  - Lines in 15°-degree steps including 45°, 90° etc.
  - Instead of an ellipse, it will draw a circle and
  - instead of a rectangle, a quadrate.

[Ctrl] = Circle, Quadrate; exact angle.

- While pressing [Shift]-Left Mouse Button
  - a started ellipse, circle or rectangle will be drawn around the first point (the first point is the middle point and not the edge point as usual) or
  - you can change the size of objects around their middle point or
  - with [Ctrl]+[Shift] together you can draw a circle or quadrate around the first point.

[Shift]= around first point.

- Usage: This way, you can draw a circle exactly around a point or axis intersection point. If you click on this point and start drawing your object, you can press and hold [Ctrl]+[Shift] while drawing.

You do not have to remember this, just try it:

- Draw an ellipse or rectangle, but keep the left mouse button pressed and then try:
  - [Ctrl] or [Shift]-Button or both?
  - You'll see the effect on the screen as soon as you move the mouse slightly!

> Press and hold the left mouse button and try!
>
> If you want to move elements with the left mouse button pressed, or copy them with an additional right-click, it helps to touch the corner so that they remain on the grid points.

9.1.1 Exercise: Quadrates and Circles with Guidelines and Grid

➢ **New Drawing** with letter crosswise, save as "Quadrates and Circles".

➢ **Draw** for the exact horizontal arrangement with a guideline (and activate "Snap to Guidelines" first):

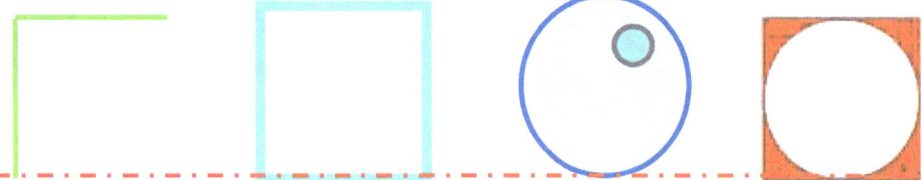

➢ For this **new drawing** use the **grid every 0.2"** and draw one quadrate, then copy it with right mouse button. With one line or some quadrates ready, you can mark and copy multiple objects at once:

Now comes a very difficult but useful exercise:

➢ The differently colored filling is produced by copying the outer, largest circle several times inwards.

  ✏ Hold down the [Shift] key so that the copied circles automatically get the same middle point.

➢ Fill each copied circle with the desired **color**.

[Shift] = Reduce or enlarge around the center point.

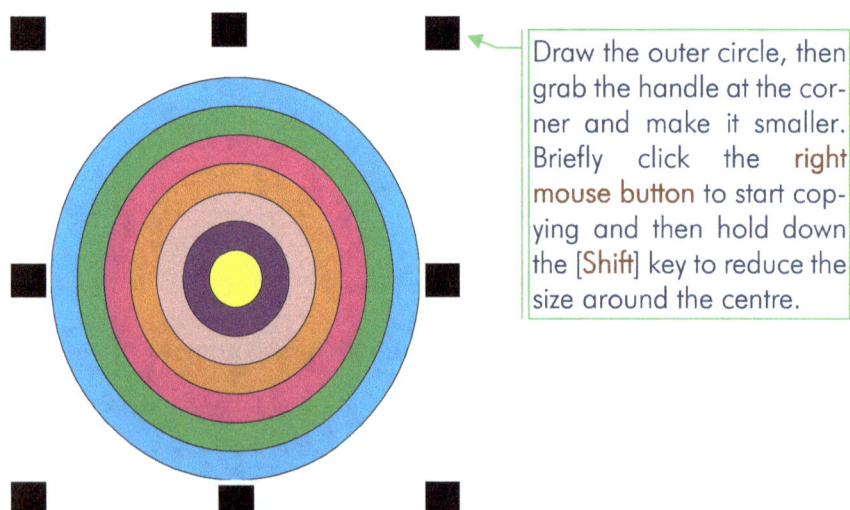

Draw the outer circle, then grab the handle at the corner and make it smaller. Briefly click the **right mouse button** to start copying and then hold down the [Shift] key to reduce the size around the centre.

This is no problem if you press the **right mouse button** during the movement + holding down **the left mouse button**, then you can at any time try pressing [Shift] or [Ctrl] to find the target position.

9.2 Polygon, Spiral, Grinding

Corel also offers special shapes, which can be found with the polygon tool under the symbols for rectangles and circles. We already touched on this briefly on pages 31 and 36, and now in a little more detail. Draw the following:

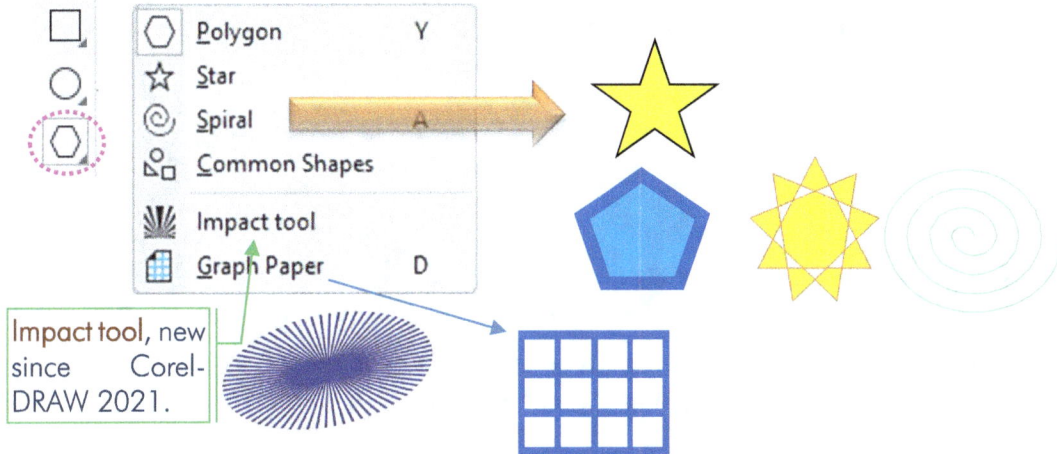

Note: Spiral and effect not included with Essentials.

9.2.1 Set-Up Polygons

Helpful:

Draw first with the default, then you can set each of these elements by mouse or in the **property bar**. Thus, e.g., triangles (=three corners), octagons or stars:

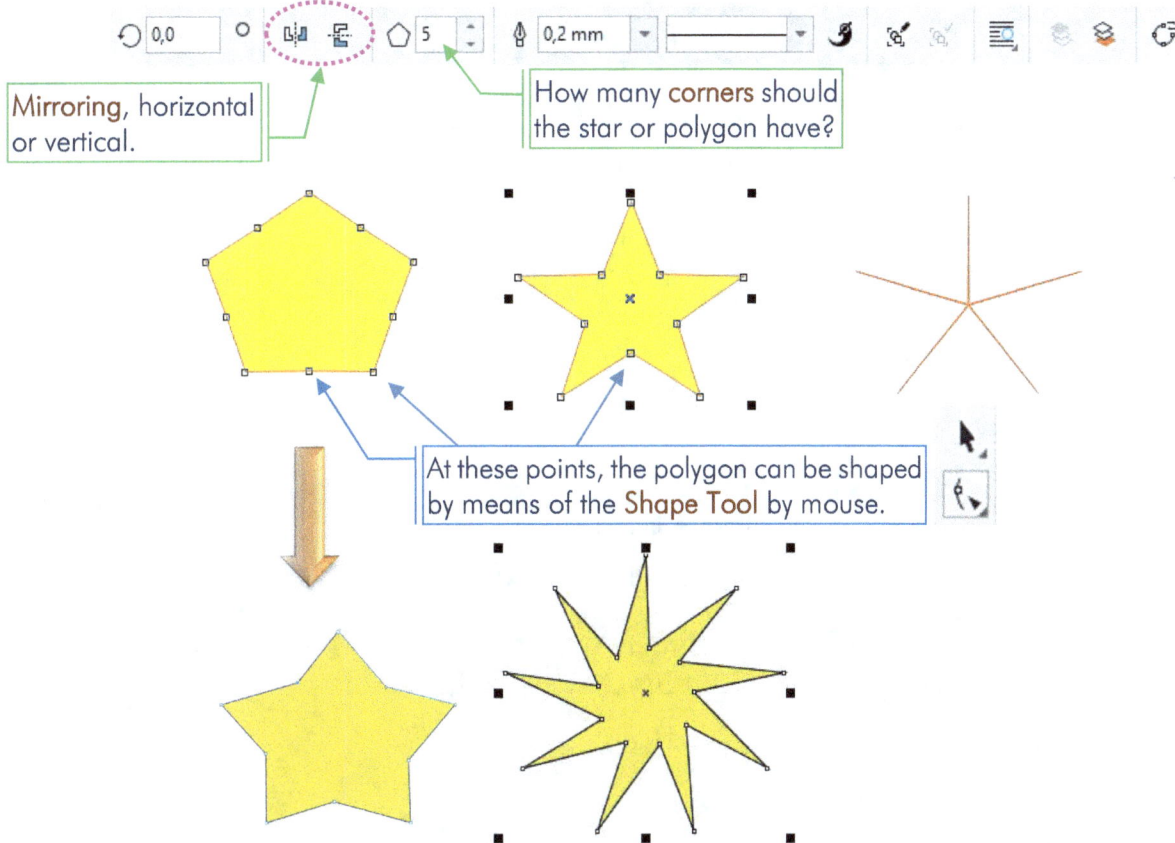

9.3 Common Shapes: Basic, Arrow, Flowchart etc.

Corel also has prefabricated standard shapes, e.g., for a flash, an arrow or various stars or speech bubbles.

> In the polygon menu, see above, you will find the Common Shapes (Basic, Arrow Flowchart etc.), too.

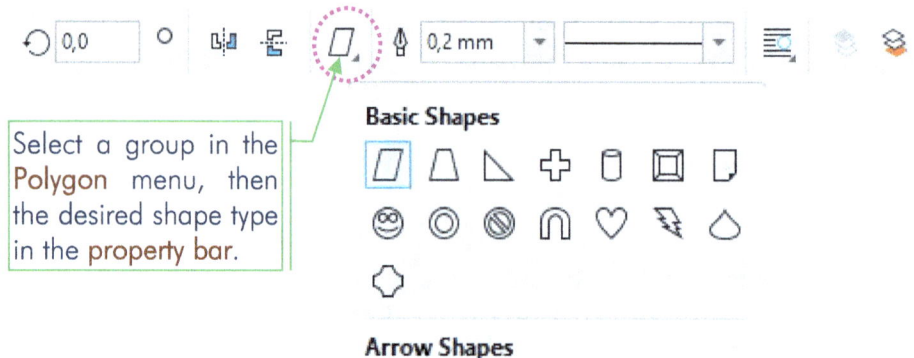

> If you have selected "Common Shapes", you can select a shape from this icon in the property bar:

Select a group in the Polygon menu, then the desired shape type in the property bar.

Of course, these shapes can also be retrofitted. Note the tap points.

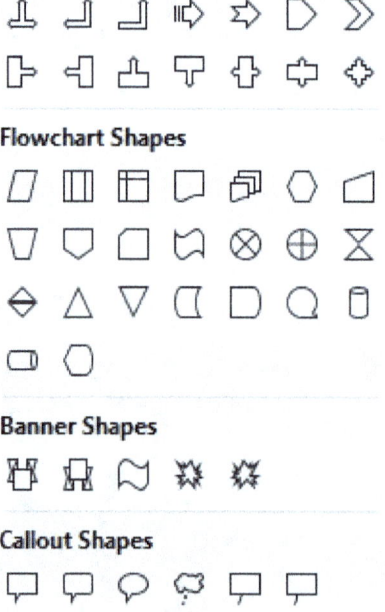

10. Ruler, Zero Point, Group

It is sometimes helpful to lay the zero point appropriately, for one wheel, for example, in the center. Or to adjust the scale from the start instead, to manually count every dimension later.

10.1 Ruler and Zero Point

In order to specify the dimensions for a drawing, a Zero point is set and is scaled up horizontally (X-axis) and vertically (Y-axis).

In a CorelDRAW Drawing you can read the coordinates on the rulers at the top and left of the screen and usually the zero point is the left bottom of the page, but depending on the drawing the zero point is sometimes better placed in the middle with 0 or lower right.

(0, 0)

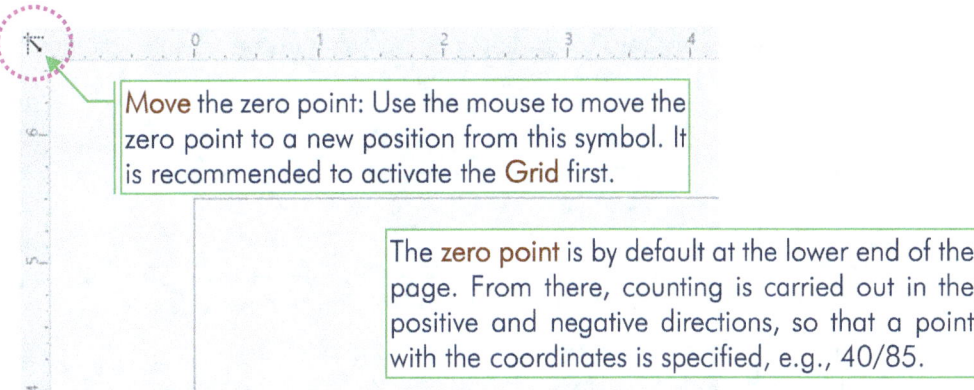

Move the zero point: Use the mouse to move the zero point to a new position from this symbol. It is recommended to activate the Grid first.

The zero point is by default at the lower end of the page. From there, counting is carried out in the positive and negative directions, so that a point with the coordinates is specified, e.g., 40/85.

- Double-clicking on the ruler displays the settings menu.
  - In this menu, you could change the unit for the ruler to meters or inches, or specify the start position (0,0) at Rulers/Origin.
  - e.g., if you enter with a paper sized DIN A5 crosswise horizontal 210 is the zero point on the right side of paper.

If you click on the menu item "Edit Scale" below at Document/Rulers, a window appears, in which you can choose other scales:

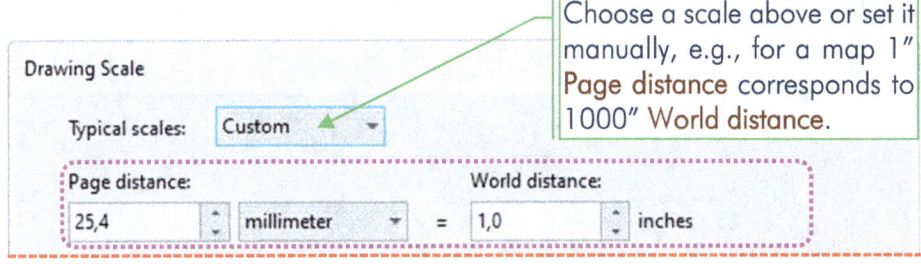

Choose a scale above or set it manually, e.g., for a map 1" Page distance corresponds to 1000" World distance.

10.2 Exercise: Railway Wheel

We want to draw a railway wheel. Preparations:

➢ Start a new drawing, choose centimeters as the units and set the size to 100x100 cm:

➢ Double-click on the ruler and set the **origin at 50, 50 cm** so that it is exactly in the center of the page.

✏ Then, use the Zoom Tool to select "Whole Page" to see the result.

➢ Place the **grid every 5 cm** (centimeters apart) and turn on the grid and guidelines.

> Attention! Corel only points at the grid points when you click or release near a point! Note the "# Grid" marking that appears.

➢ Set a horizontal **Guideline** at 0 and a vertical at 0 because the origin 0/0 is now in the center of the page.

Drawing is easier now with the guidelines and grid:

➢ Draw a large circle: Set the starting point exactly in the middle, then draw the circle while pressing **[Ctrl]+[Shift]-Button** around this middle point.

➢ We cannot simply draw the smaller circle, since we could move the first circle. Therefore, we copy the first circle and reduce it:

✏ Touch and hold down the corner handles, right-click for copying, press [Shift], locate the target position and release the mouse.

✏ Mark both circles, then **combine** them and choose a filling color.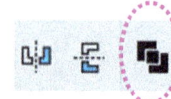

➢ Just as the **small axis circles** can be drawn, combining would not be necessary here since both circles can be filled simply in color if the smaller circle is at the front.

➢ Now draw the first horizontal spoke and place it at the back. If necessary, switch off the grid using [Ctrl]-Y.

The first spoke is copied while rotating:

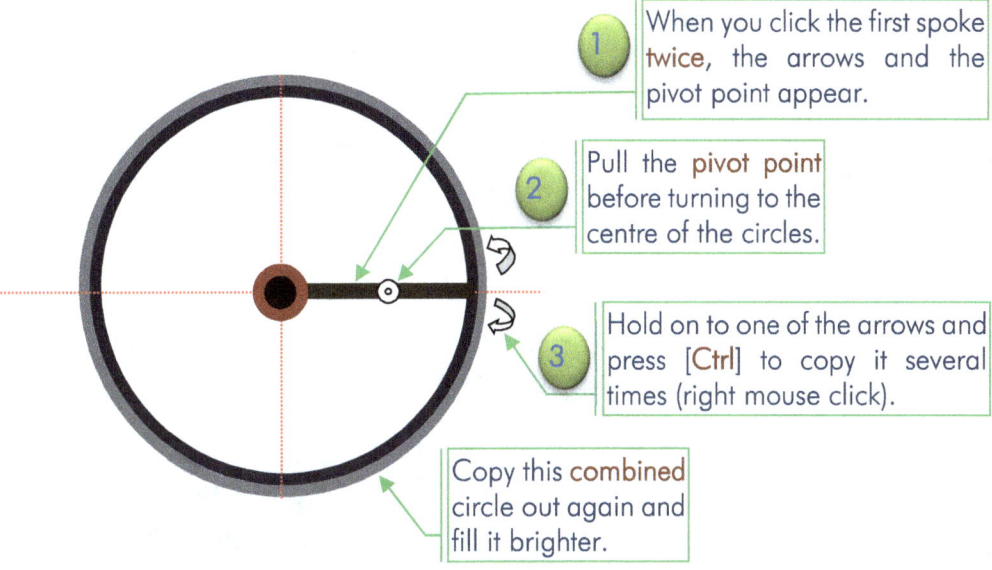

1. When you click the first spoke twice, the arrows and the pivot point appear.
2. Pull the pivot point before turning to the centre of the circles.
3. Hold on to one of the arrows and press [Ctrl] to copy it several times (right mouse click).

Copy this combined circle out again and fill it brighter.

10.3 The Menu "Transform"

[Alt]-F7

Actions with the mouse go quickly, but those elements can be inadvertently moved just as quickly. If you want to be more precise, you can use the Transformation Menu Window/Dockers/Transform:

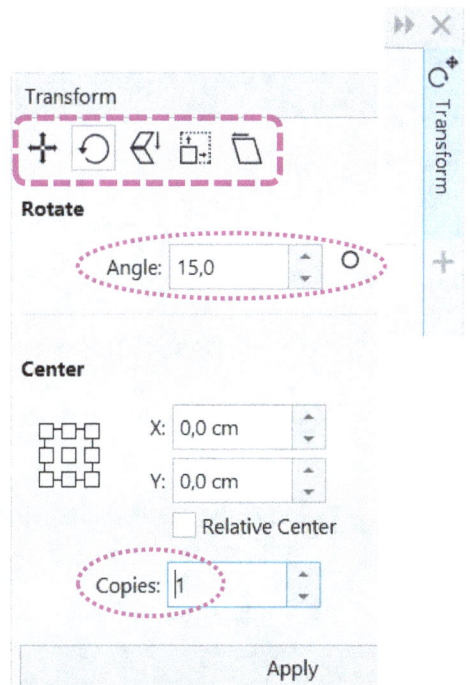

You can use the different map types to perform all actions as with the mouse, except that you enter exact coordinates here. This offers two advantages:

- It is more comfortable and you can undo all actions here, even after you have executed numerous other commands. An example:
  - It can be drawn without accidentally moving a background - it can temporarily be moved by 300mm to the side edge –
  - when everything is done, the background is reset by -300mm.

Perfectly draw the railway wheel:

- Use the Undo to erase the rotated spokes from the exercise using the mouse, then rotate the first spoke (the center of rotation is already in the center of the wheel) with the Transform-Menu.
  - If the angle of rotation does not fit evenly, reverse and try again with a different angle. How often to copy? Try or e.g., 360 ° / 15 ° = 24 - 1, so that not twice at the starting point.

Add rivets:

The rotation works so well that we can rotate same way some rivets Looks extremely difficult, but it's actually quite easy with the Edit menu.

The Target:

Draw one rivet as a radial filled circle and copy it the same way as the spokes with Transform-Menu around the wheel.

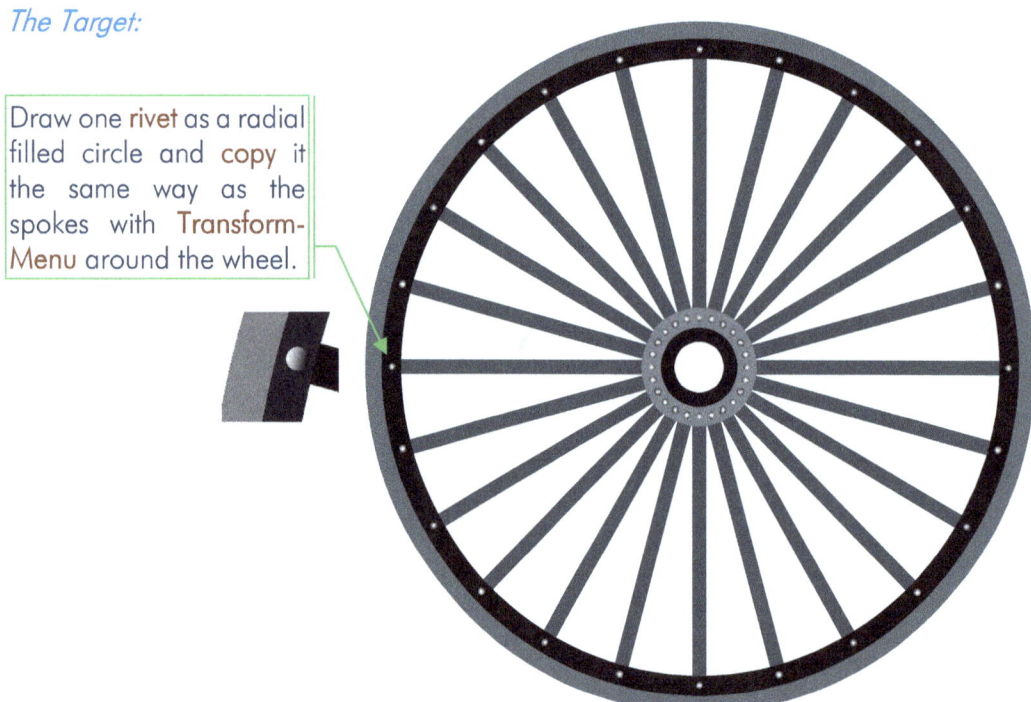

The Way:

- Draw with a high zoom one rivet as a radial filled circle.

- Move the rotation point in the middle and copy around the wheel. Oops, that was easy.

- In the same way, at high magnification, create the rivets of the wheel axle.

- Afterwards, mark all with a big selection frame or [Ctrl]-A and Group all Objects.

- Save as "railway wheel" because we'll need it later to copy into our drawing of the train.

10.4 GROUP OBJECTS

Complex drawings are not a problem if they are divided into small groups. As soon as a wheel is finished, for example, this can be grouped into one element and can then be duplicated as often as required.

Advantages of Grouping:

- Easy to **copy** or move because only one object needs to be selected.
- There is no more danger of **inadvertently moving** or deleting a small part like a rivet while you continue tracing.

Different ways of Grouping:

- You can group by symbol in the property bar (far right), in the menu (Object/Group...) or with the shortcut [Ctrl]-G.
  - ↳ Grouping is only possible if several elements have been selected.
  - ↳ If "Ungroup" is active instead of Grouping, the actual marked has already been grouped.

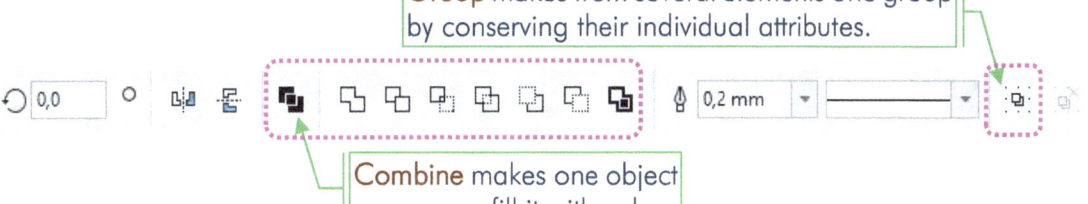

Group makes from several elements one group by conserving their individual attributes.

Combine makes one object so you can fill it with color.

If you want to edit an element of a group again:

- While holding down the [Ctrl] key, single elements can be selected from a group and edited individually.
  - ↳ For example, to assign a different color, you must release the [Ctrl] key to pick the color.
- Or you could **un-group**, edit items as usual, and then re-group them. The latter is recommended for extensive modifications.

10.4.1 EXERCISE: BLOSSOM

We'll do a similar exercise to the railway wheel, but this one may be easier.

➢ We want to draw a blossom: new drawing, draw a **circle** in the middle and one **ellipse** as the first petal.

➢ **Rotate** the ellipse like petals around the flower. Before turning, push the **center of rotation** into the middle.

➢ Then, **mark** and group everything with a large selection frame or [Ctrl]-A.

➢ While holding down the [Ctrl] key, select individual petals from the group and change the color.

The circle in the middle was set to the **back**.

11. Text and Symbols

11.1 Text Editing in Corel

➢ Start a new drawing crosswise, then choose the text-editing tool (A).

Now you have to tell the computer where you want to place the text., because we are using a drawing program, not a text program, and can put the text anywhere.

➢ Click on the desired location in the drawing and write: "Sample Text"

➢ Copy this sample text sometimes as training material. You can copy text similar to other objects this way:

★ Use the Pick Tool to move, and then copy it multiple times using the right mouse button.

11.1.1 Text Formatting with the Property Bar

The easiest way to format the text, as in a word processor, is with the Property Bar.

➢ When you click a text, you will find these icons for text formatting in the feature bar:

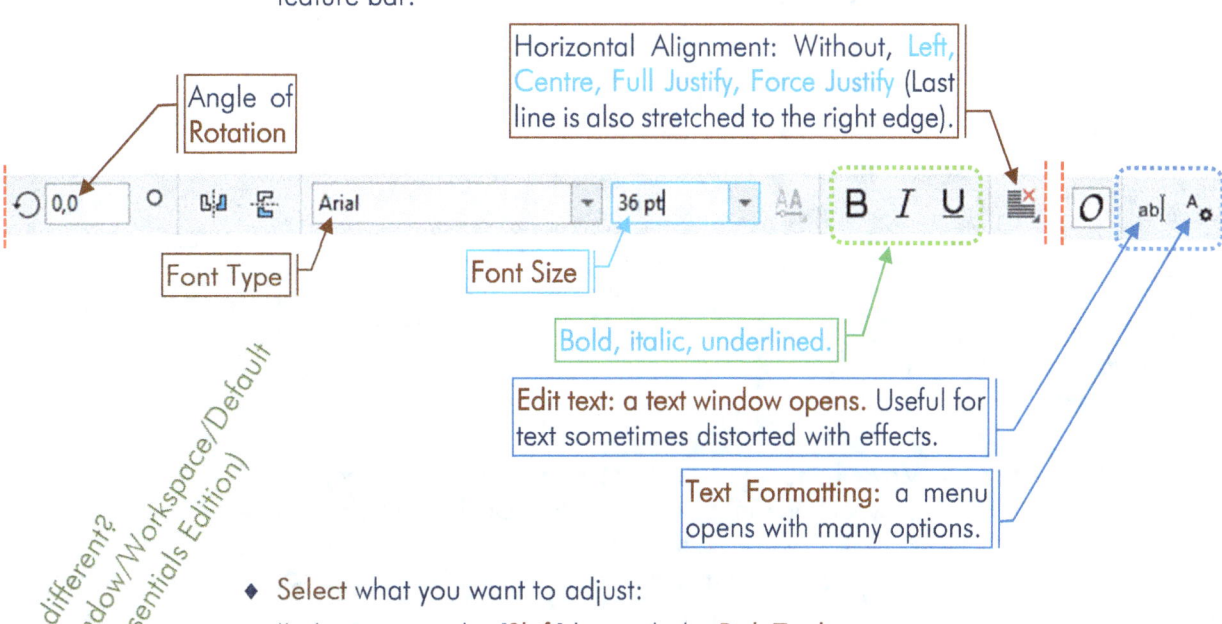

Looks different? Use Window/Workspace/Default (not by Essentials Edition)

♦ Select what you want to adjust:
  ✋ by pressing the [Shift] key with the Pick Tool,
  ✋ Or by pressing the left mouse button within a text with the Text Tool.

11.1.2 Modify Text with the Pick Tool

When you finish the text editing, the **text is an object** like a rectangle or line, so you can edit the text as well:

- Click on the text with the **Pick Tool** once:
  - to change the **text size at the Handle Points** or
  - to catch the text and move it to another position (try to click on the text body, not on a handle point) or
  - Click while moving the right mouse button for copying.
- Click on the text with the **Pick Tool** a second time and you can:

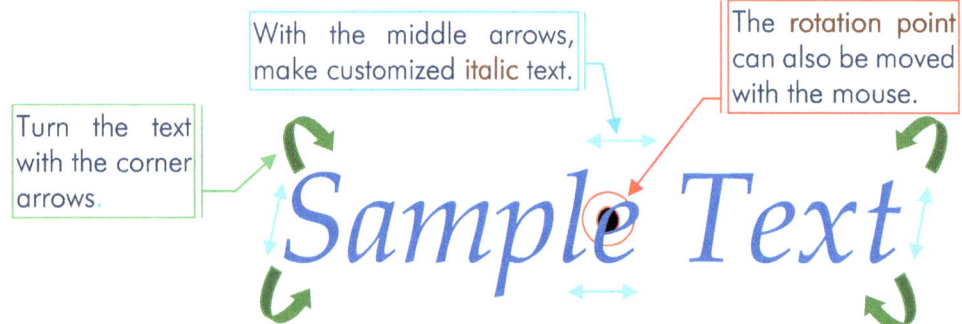

That's how it should be:

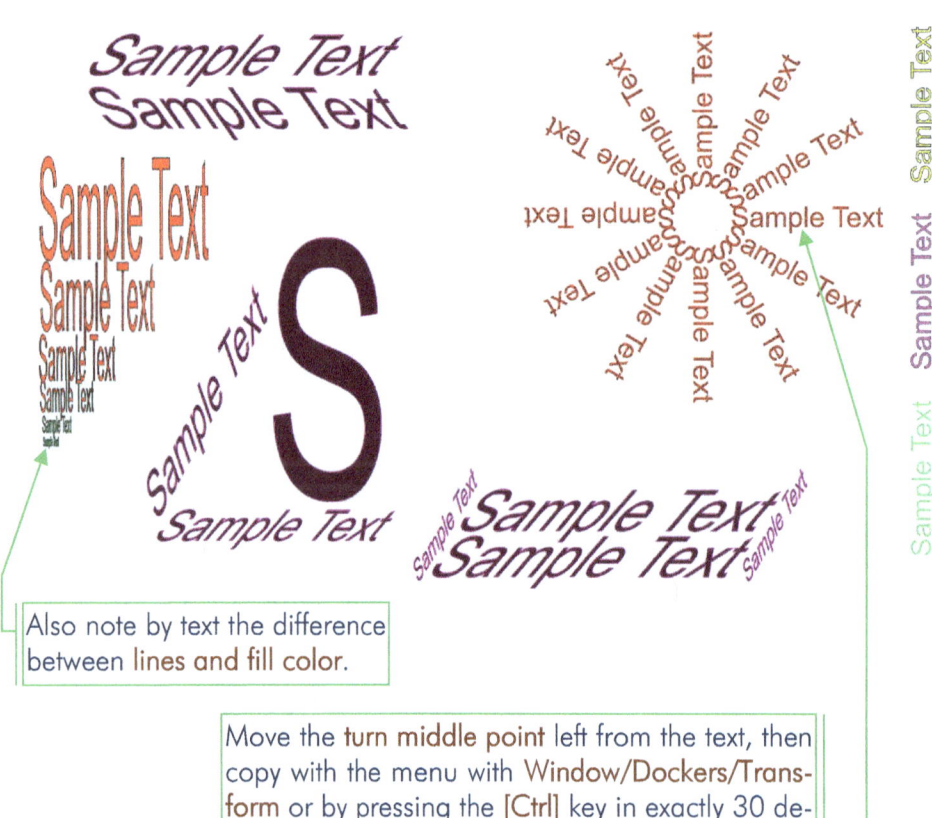

Double clicking on text switches to the Text Tool!

11.2 Exercise: Solar

To complete the basics for drawing, let's try an exercise with lines, a circle and text. Draw the following letterhead before setting up grids and guide lines:

Preparation:

- New Drawing, *set page with* 80x50mm or if you prefer inch 30"x20", set Grid suitable, two Guidelines and activate Snap On.

Circle and Lines:

- Draw the Circle ([Ctrl] key) for the sun with yellow filling and line.
- Draw the first vertical line:
  - Click two times on this line (not a double-click) and move the center point to the center of the sun.
  - Now you can copy each turn with right mouse button click and press the [Ctrl] key on the lines each 15°.
- Draw the rectangle for the solar module and rotate and arrange it appropriately to shorten the solar beams.

Corner Rounding:

- For the rounding of the corners, you can find these controls in the Properties bar:

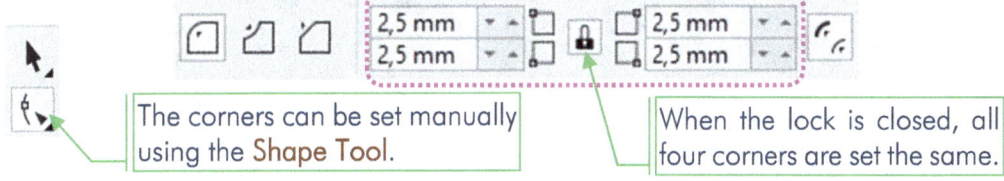

The corners can be set manually using the Shape Tool.

When the lock is closed, all four corners are set the same.

- Write the text and format it centered, place two rectangles as a background and fill it appropriately.
  - Use the grid or the coordinate fields in the property bar to set the rectangles to exact coordinates so you can place the text perfectly in the middle of it.

| 20.0 mm |
| 10.0 mm |
| 2,5 " |
| 1,0 " |

- Mark all with [Ctrl]-A or a big mark rectangle and group it – so it is useable as letterhead. .
  - Copy it into your word processing program as letterhead in the header. You can export in CorelDRAW as a wmf or png-file for the best compatibility with MS Office programs. Also note the option of only exporting selected elements.

11.3 THE SYMBOL FONTS

The content of Windows and the Corel program package are special fonts that contain pictures instead of letters. Of these fonts only examples were installed on your computer, as every installed font occupy memory.

♦ New exercise: the **menu for symbol fonts** can be opened with **[Ctrl]-[F11]** or **Text/Glyphs**.

On the right side, a docker appears:

With these arrows ▶▶ the toolbar can be displayed or hidden; with the **X** you can switch off the docker.

Choose the font here.
It is recommended to browse through the pages for the first time to check which fonts are available (note Webdings and Wingdings).

Either use the mouse to **drag** the desired symbol into the drawing
--- or ---
click on the symbol, "**Copy**" below and then paste it into the drawing. The latter also goes into a text with the text tool if the cursor is at the desired place in the text when you paste it.

Interesting fonts: **Yu Gothic** and **MS Reference Specialty** with fractions and special characters, **Wingdings, Webdings, Symbol**, fonts with Chinese characters: **MingLiU** and **MS JhengHei**.

Notice the **scroll bar** on the right for even more selection.

Integrate a symbol into a text:

These special characters can also be inserted into a text from this Corel menu: if the text is opened with the text tool (cursor flashes at the desired location), double-click on the character you want to insert.

Then, the special character is inserted into the text, consequently just as a normal letter moves and changes e.g., with the font size.

Only the font can't be changed afterwards because the new font also applies to the special character. If it is necessary to change the font type of the text, then reinsert the symbol or reassign the character font to the symbol.

After inserting the object correctly with the **Shape Tool**, the letter distance should match up.

Third Part

Fillings, ClipArt, Photos

Basics Color Models:

- CMYK: the color model used by offset printing and every four-color printer. It means: C=CYAN, M=MAGENTA, Y=YELLOW, K=BLAC**K**.
- RGB is the color scheme of every monitor and TV. All colors are mixed from the base colors RED, GREEN and BLUE.
  - ☞ RGB is a so named **additive color scheme**, because all colors together result in white (light is mixed), while by CMYK all colors together result in black, all colors off in white (= **subtractive scheme**).

12. Single Fillings

12.1 Overview select Filling and Adjust

- You can choose colors from the color palette directly on the right:
  - Select the object and change the fill color with the left mouse button, and the line color with the right one.
- For more precise color selection or special color fillings, there are two options by this symbol in the Tool Bar:

Interactive fill tool: Click on the object, then "Interactive Fill", then select a fill option in the property bar at the top.

12.2 Overview of Fillings

Type:	Sample:
No fill / turn off fill	
Solid fill	
Gradient fill: Color transitions between two colors or across multiple colors.	
Full color pattern fill = different color patterns are selectable.	
Special fills (bitmap pattern fill, two-color pattern fill, fill pattern, postscript) follow in chapter 14.	

12.3 THE COLOR PALETTE

> Open the Pyramid Squares exercise from p. 50 so that you can try out what has been described.

> Open some more color palettes by Window/Dockers or Color Palettes/Palettes, under Process/Pantone and Spot the interesting pallets can be found.

> Close all open palettes but not the Default palette. You can close unmark by Window/Color Palettes/Palettes or by this arrow at top of the pallet:

Close a palette by this arrow and then Palette/Close.

If you want to select many colors, it is convenient to drag the color palette into the center of the drawing.

So, colors can choose easy:

Hold at these points and pull them to the centre, then adjust the window size at the edges or corners.

Back: pull at the top of the bar, and drag with the mouse to the right edge of the window until the color-coded position frame appears. Easier, if you close all dockers windows before.

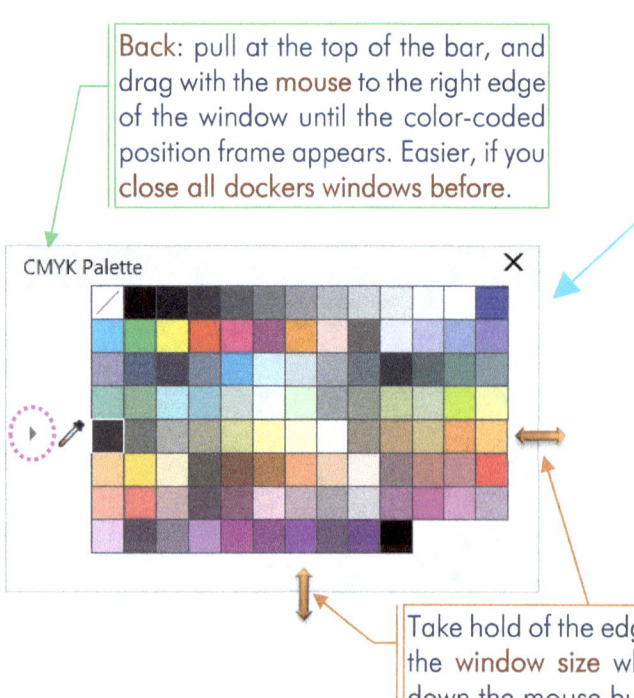

Take hold of the edges to adjust the window size while holding down the mouse button.

- Under Window/Color Palettes you will find interesting commands for palettes, e.g., a new palette can be created from the colors used in the current graphic or all open palettes can be hidden again with Close all Palettes, in order to then show a desired palette again.

Instead of using the palettes, you can also set each color manually, which follows in the next chapter.

12.4 Color Settings

You can also choose a color as you like on this way:

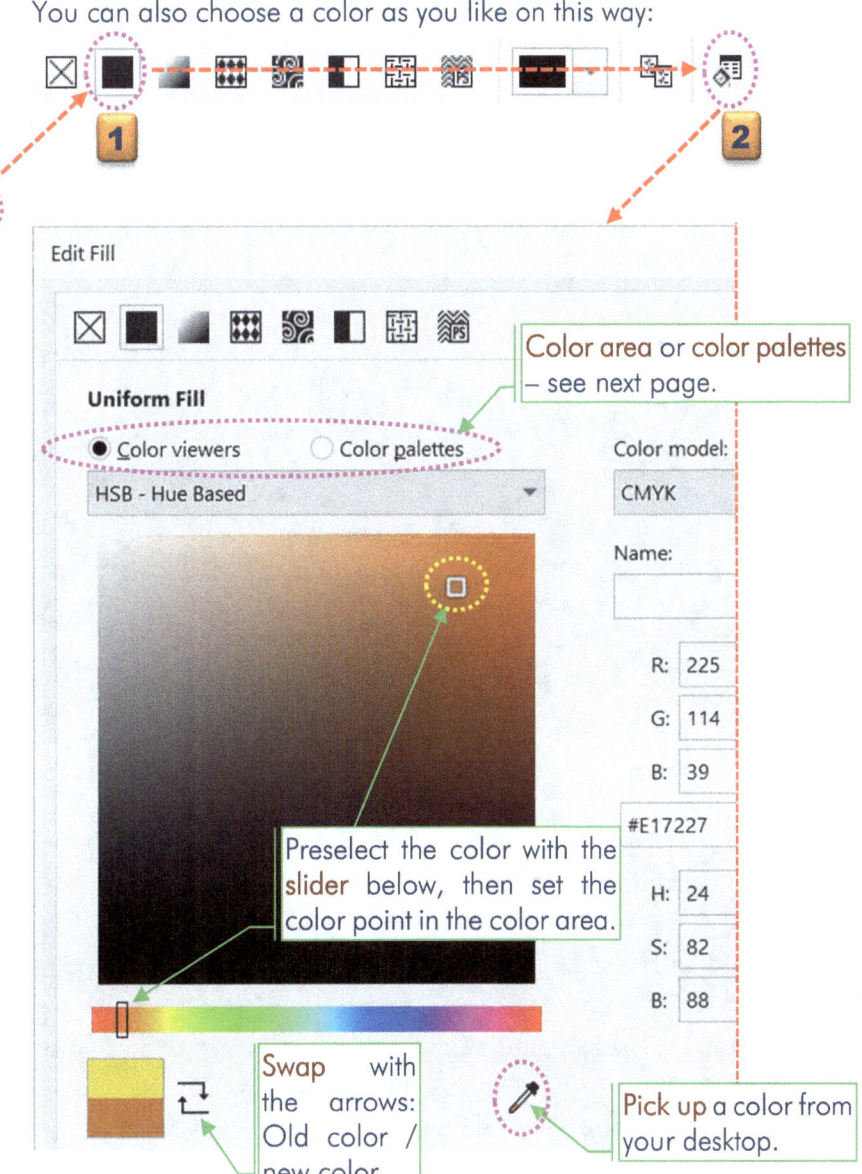

Color area or color palettes – see next page.

Preselect the color with the **slider** below, then set the color point in the color area.

Swap with the **arrows**: Old color / new color.

Pick up a color from your desktop.

Use the mouse to set colors directly on the object:

In the case of **single-color fillings**, the color can be selected from the color palette on the right using the mouse; in the case of multi-colored fillings, an adjustment arrow appears when you click on it.

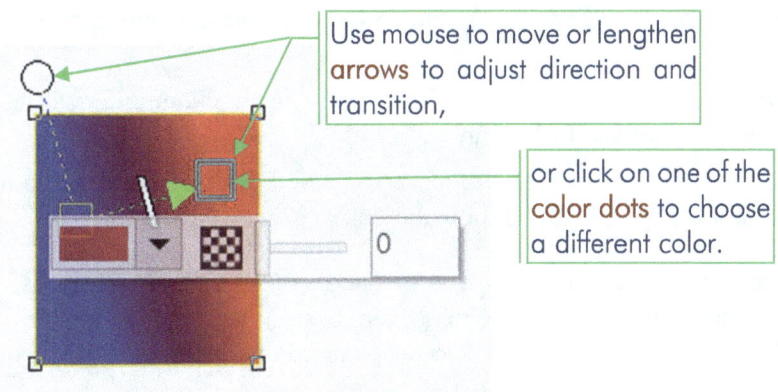

Use mouse to move or lengthen **arrows** to adjust direction and transition,

or click on one of the **color dots** to choose a different color.

12.5 Color Palettes

CorelDRAW has some color palettes. Switch to the palettes in the previous menu:

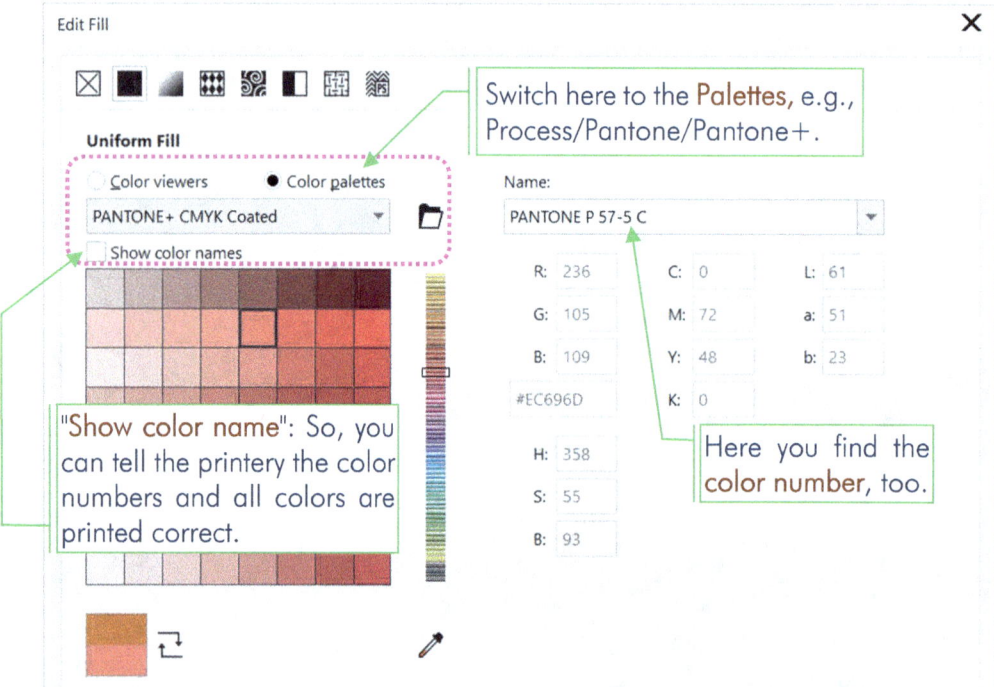

About the Palettes:

- **Palettes** are standardized color catalogues used by **painters and printers**, so that colors can be accurately reproduced, e.g.:
- Colors according to the **Focoltone**, a scheme you use when you paint your rawhide wallpaper.
- **Pantone** colors are the standard in graphics and printing, and are also used for interior decoration, cosmetics and product design.
- The printers and painters have **catalogs** of these color palettes and can thus reproduce exactly the desired color.
- By **Window/Color Palettes** you find all commands for color palettes, here you could also create your own palette.

The palettes are very important when a color needs to be exactly reproduced:

- If you change the painter or the printing company, the stationery letterhead or the business card can be printed again in exactly the same colors.
  - ↪ If you use the palette colors in Corel and specify the numbers to the printer, the colors fit as planned.
  - ↪ It is ideal if you use a **printed color palette catalogue** because your monitor and printer don't show the colors exactly the same.

> The use of the color palettes allows **identical colors** on business cards, letterheads, company signs, painting, etc. Depending on your version, CorelDRAW does not have all or other palettes available.

12.6 Smart Fill Tool

Smart Fill Tool: specify a fill and line color and then click on the area to be filled. Smart, because cut surfaces are recognized automatically. With Smart Fill, you can have cut surfaces filled.

➢ Draw a rectangle and circle and try it out.

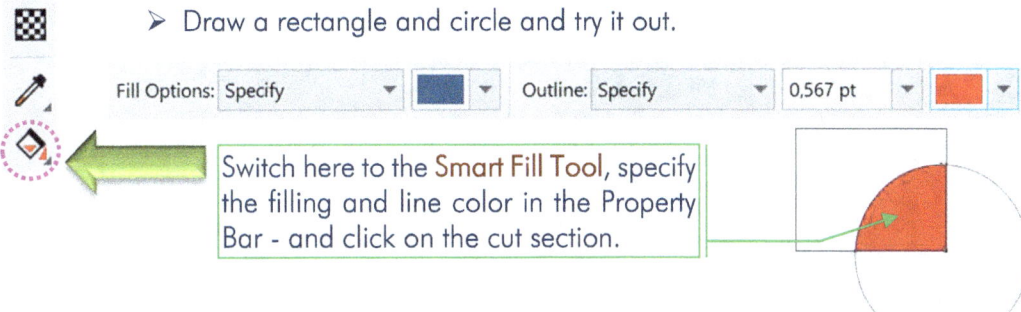

Switch here to the Smart Fill Tool, specify the filling and line color in the Property Bar - and click on the cut section.

Set fill and line (outline) colors:

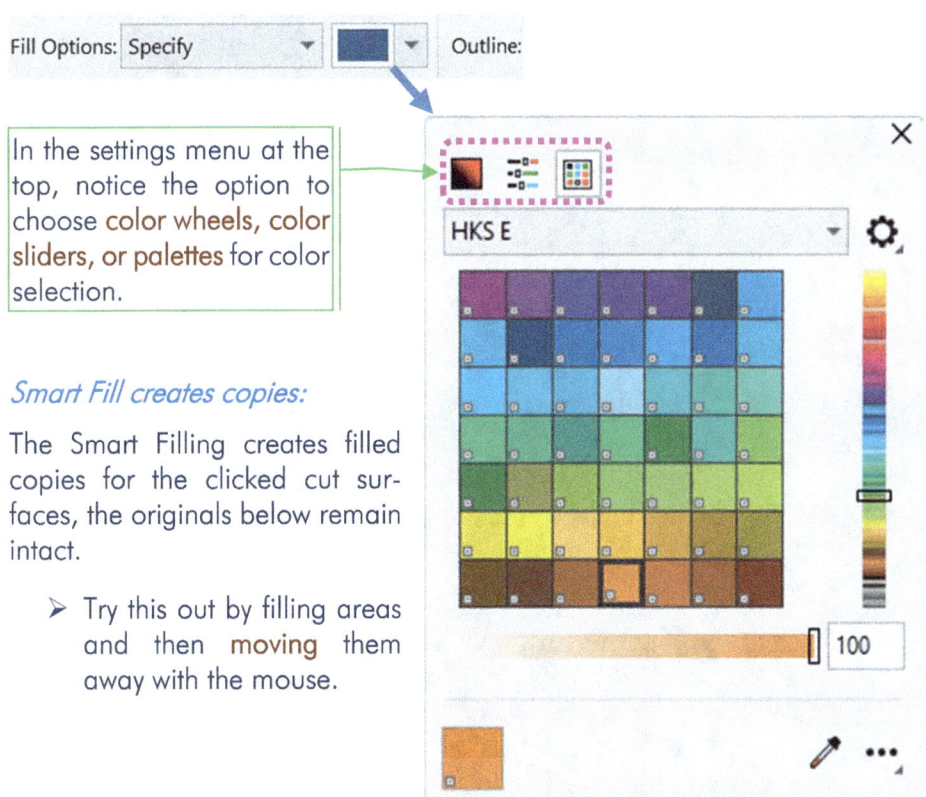

In the settings menu at the top, notice the option to choose color wheels, color sliders, or palettes for color selection.

Smart Fill creates copies:

The Smart Filling creates filled copies for the clicked cut surfaces, the originals below remain intact.

➢ Try this out by filling areas and then moving them away with the mouse.

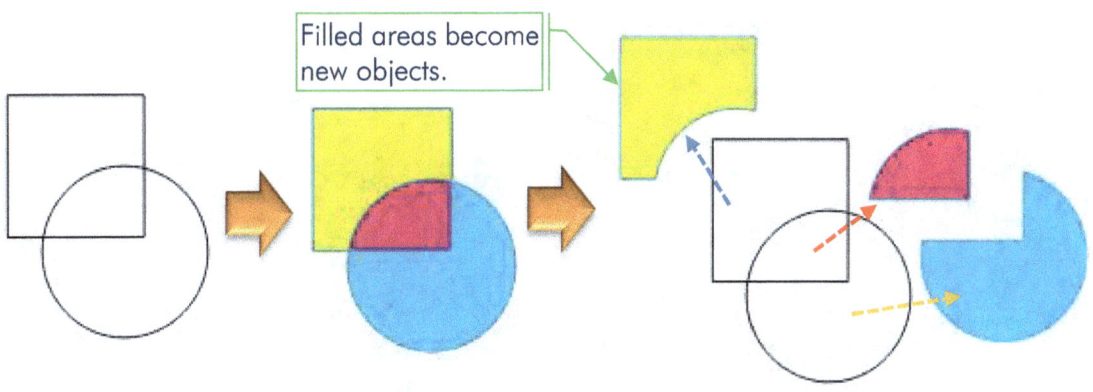

Filled areas become new objects.

13. FOUNTAIN FILL

Color Gradient Fillings are nice and versatile.

> Open the exercise "Pyramids Squares" (s. P. 50) and choose the "Interactive Fill Tool".

Now we choose the next option, "Fountain Fill":

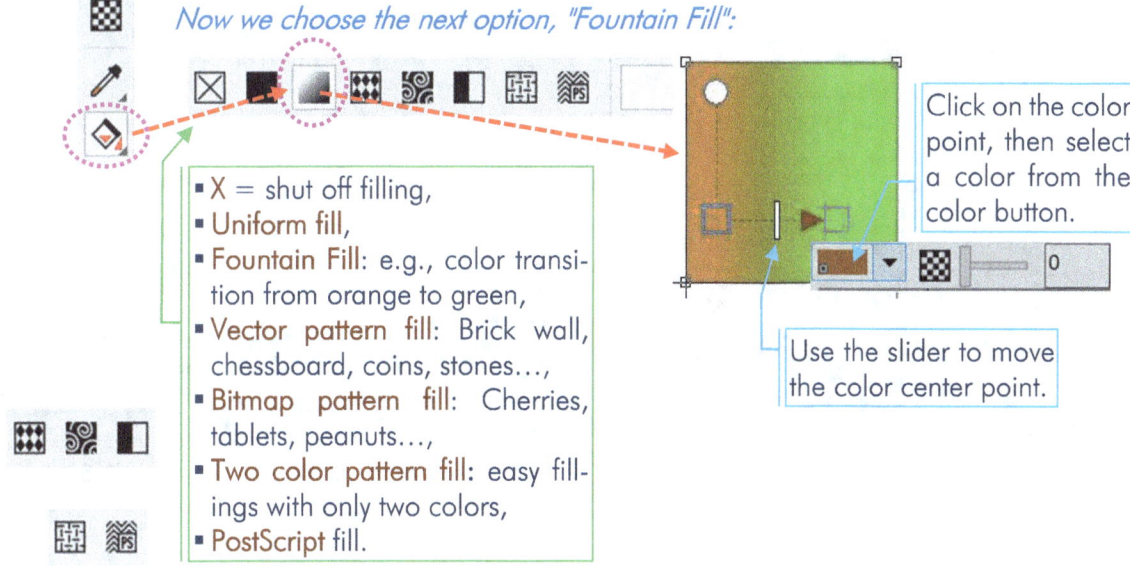

- X = shut off filling,
- Uniform fill,
- Fountain Fill: e.g., color transition from orange to green,
- Vector pattern fill: Brick wall, chessboard, coins, stones…,
- Bitmap pattern fill: Cherries, tablets, peanuts…,
- Two color pattern fill: easy fillings with only two colors,
- PostScript fill.

Click on the color point, then select a color from the color button.

Use the slider to move the color center point.

In these next exercises, you can try various filling types in each square:

Text can fill, too.

Exercise Pyramids Squares

LINDEMANN GROUP © MSC. (UAS) PETER SCHIESSL

13.1 Adjust the Fountain Fill

You can change a fill at any time. Let's try it. The fountain fill should be at the -37° angle.

> Choose the **Interactive Fill Tool**, then click on a new rectangle and **edit the fill** in the property bar on the right-most symbol:

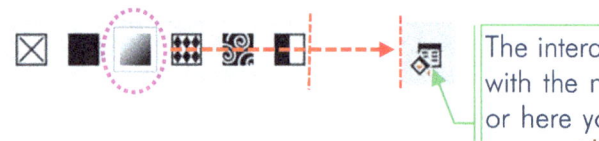

The interactive fill could be adjusted with the mouse, in the Property bar or here you can open the following menu with all the options for fillings.

Here in the menu, you can easily set up the filling:

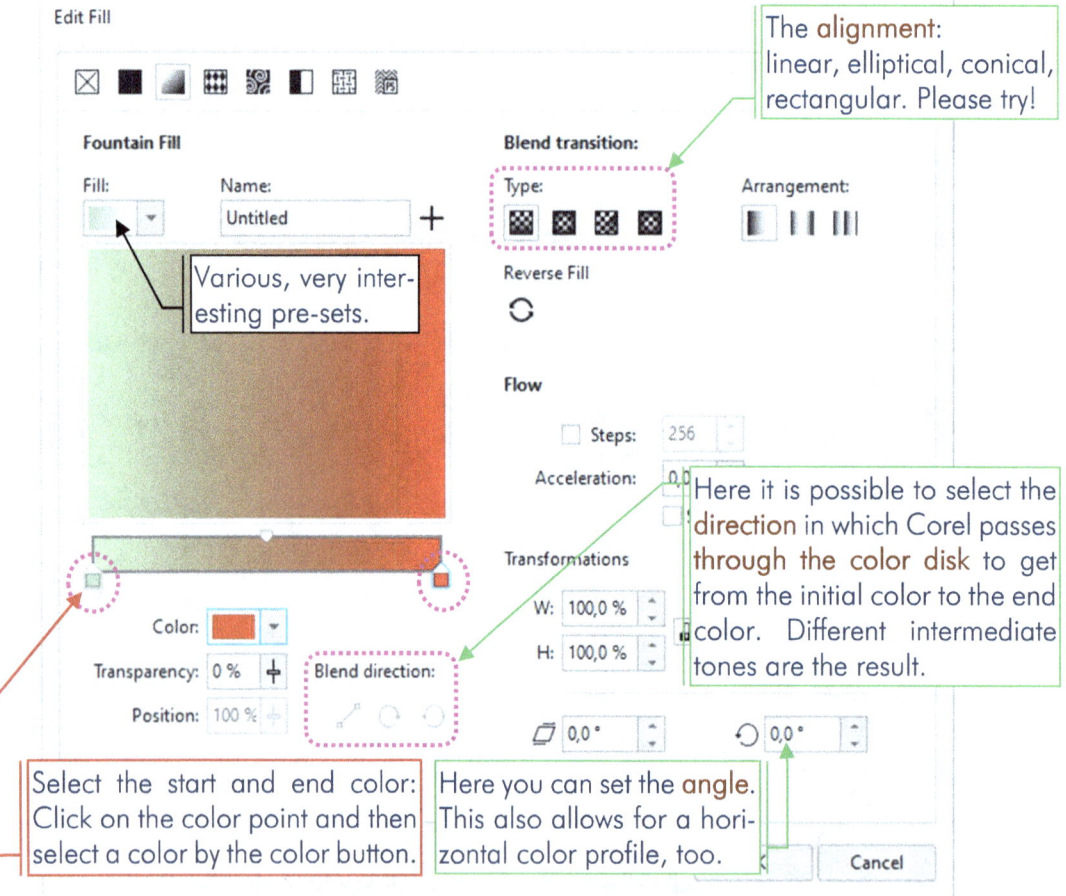

The **alignment**: linear, elliptical, conical, rectangular. Please try!

Various, very interesting pre-sets.

Here it is possible to select the **direction** in which Corel passes through the **color disk** to get from the initial color to the end color. Different intermediate tones are the result.

Select the start and end color: Click on the color point and then select a color by the color button.

Here you can set the **angle**. This also allows for a horizontal color profile, too.

The Alignment:

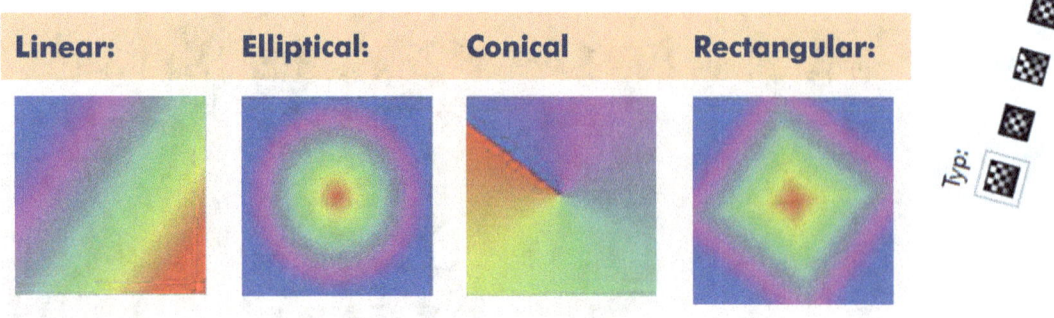

| Linear: | Elliptical: | Conical: | Rectangular: |

> Try different fountain fillings and set them to some squares of the exercise.

13.2 Multiple Color Filling

With these settings for the color profile, see previous page, a two-color or multi-color filling can also be achieved.

Set up the color gradient filling:

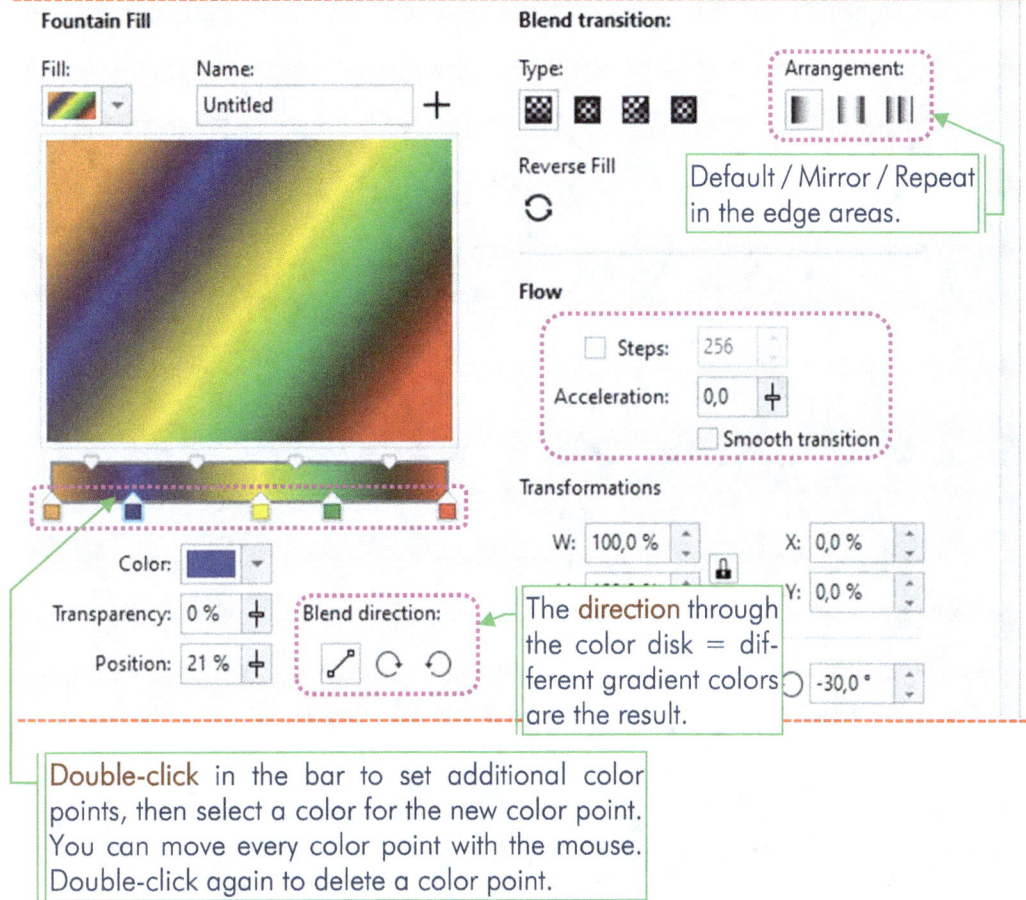

Double-click in the bar to set additional color points, then select a color for the new color point. You can move every color point with the mouse. Double-click again to delete a color point.

- The initial and final colors can also be selected on the square boxes at the left and right end of the bar.
- Any number of additional color points can be set. For each point a color can be determined.
- Color points can be moved with the mouse.

The preset 256 color streaks cause smooth transitions, since the fine stripes are not visible. Multi-strips cause unnecessary computational overhead, but sometimes it is desirable to deliberately reduce the number of strips so that the individual color strips become visible, e.g., to draw a flag.

- Here you can set any number of strips. Try to reduce it from 256 to e.g., 60 or 6.
- By Transformations, the size of the color gradient can be set, at 80% the 20% at the edge remains with the start and end color.

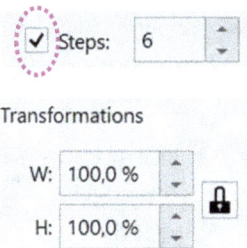

- If you have a **border area** in this area:
  - **Default:** the start and end color
  - **Repeat & Mirror:** the fountain fill starts again, mirrored.
  - **Reverse:** the fountain fill starts again from the start to end color.

| Default | Repeat & Mirror | Reverse |

13.3 Exercise: Christmas Card

An easy exercise with many color gradient fillings:

> Use the format **Japanese Postcard crosswise:**

Draw a tree with the polyline (by pen):

> With the **Polyline,** click once for the next line, double-click to stop. Draw roughly from the end to the starting point.   ✎ Polylinie
  - With the Essentials edition there is no polyline, then simply draw with the normal line: double-click to continue.

> Then, choose the **Shape Tool** and correctly move the points until it becomes like a Christmas tree.

> Finally, set a green fill.

The tree trunk and the jewelry:

- Paint the **trunk** (freehand line) with a brown filling, then set **backwards** - so you can draw the trunk higher and so the section does not match exactly.

- Finally draw the **jewelry** as filled circles once, then copy several times. Ideal: radial or rectangular color filling or a preset.

> Draw with **Freehand Line**: double-click draws further, one click stops or as **Polyline (not by Essentials)**: single click draws further, double-click stops.

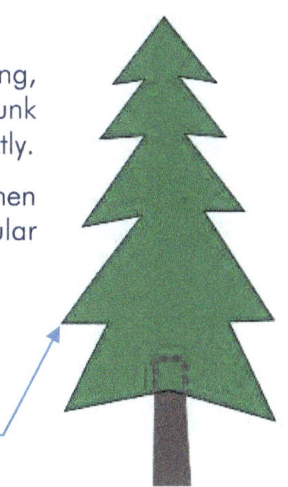

Group and duplicate the Christmas tree:

- **Mark** the tree with a bigger mark rectangle using the **Pick Tool** and **group it** (with symbol or Object/Group).

  - Now as a group you can easily copy the tree by clicking the right mouse button while moving it to another side.

The Gifts:

- Draw the **gifts**, each with a different fill and line color as filled rectangles.

- Place the gifts **forward or backward** accordingly. Finally, group the gifts.

- We have used a basic form, can be selected from the hexagon symbol. It would be nicer if you searched in the web for a clipart.

Text and background:

- Write the **Text** as usual with the **Text tool** and move it to the right position with the mouse. For an exact position you can use the coordinate fields in the Property bar,

- Set a rectangle with fountain fill and rounded edges behind the text on the top,

- Use the **Polygon tool** and find the **Banner shapes**.

- Use it to draw a **big rectangle** with same dimensions as the paper, set it in the background, and format it with a fountain fill.

Notes: ....

....

....

....

....

13.4 Exercise: Carton Home

Create a template for a door sign.

Prepare drawing:

- New file, page format DIN A5 high or letter high. Set a grid width of 5mm and align to grid.

- Set guidelines as edge boundaries.

Copy the rectangles:

- Draw the first rectangle and adjust it in size.

- Complete the first row by copying. If necessary, delete it again and change the size of the first rectangle.

- Make a group out of the first line, then copy this line twice downward.

- Make a group of the first block again and copy a second time downward right.

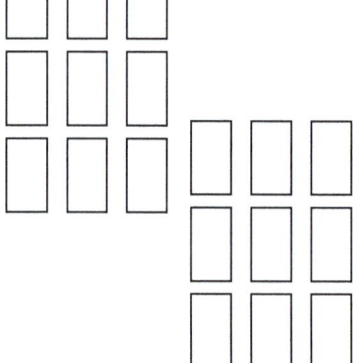

- Mark all and set a matching fountain fill with an angle (see next page).

  ✎ Aslant fountain fills are very nice most of the time but the direction should be not right down, but top right.

- Complete the text, write "Carton-", click elsewhere, and write "home", click on another place and write "Manufacture".

- Now you can set these three graphic texts to the guideline on the left side and expand to the guideline on the right side. At last, expand it above to set the height.

  ✎ If finished, mark the text and set a matching fountain fill.

- Complete it with the address block left bottom. Copy the filling.

- Mark all text and add a Drop Shadow (by Essentials not available) and choose in the Property bar the preset Medium Glow. In the Property bar you can choose a nice color for the shadow:

➢ Finish the exercise with a rectangle the same size as the paper and a fountain fill as the background. Here we use a **conical-reverse fountain fill**:

Looks different? Use Window-Workspace-Default (not by Essentials Edition)

13.5 EXERCISE: STEAM LOCOMOTIVE

This drawing is already challenging in a course with support, but it is a good exercise that shows that it is not so difficult to create complex drawings.

➢ **New file**, switch the units to meters and then set **30 meters long and 10 meters high**. Display the whole page and set the grid to 0.2m each and activate "Snap on grid".

➢ Almost all (locomotive, windows, wagons …) are simply drawn from **rectangles**, which were filled in color:

↳ Locomotives with **color gradient** type linear "black-white-black" horizontally, thus rotated by 90 °, chimneys with the same color gradient vertically, see page 78).

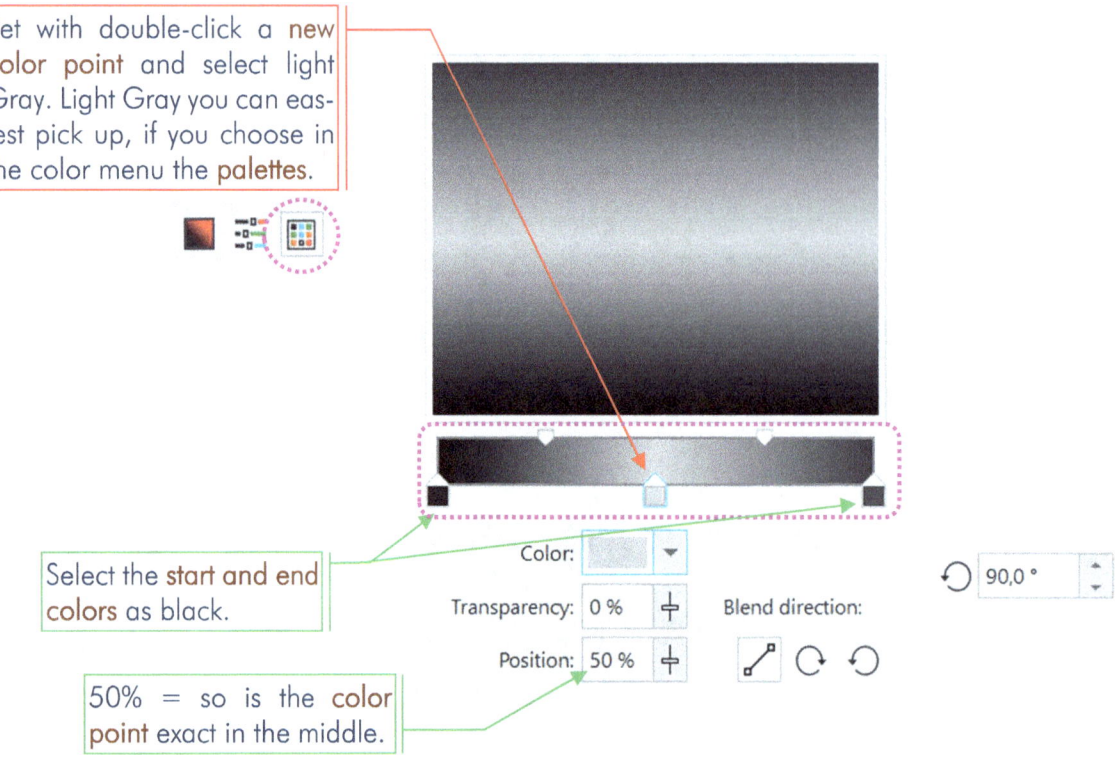

- Use the **polygon tool** for the tip, the stars and the first chimney, each adjusting the number of corners.
- We already created a wheel in a separate drawing; the exercise can be found on page 60. **Copy the wheel** in this drawing and duplicate it horizontally by pressing the [Shift] button.
- For the **background**, draw two large rectangles, fill the upper with blue color, and fill the lower green and place backwards (property bar).
- Draw the smoke **clouds** with the freehand line. For this, switch off the grid and release the mouse only if you have reached again the starting point so that the figure is **closed** and can be filled.

14. Special Fillings

To illustrate, some examples, which is presented below:

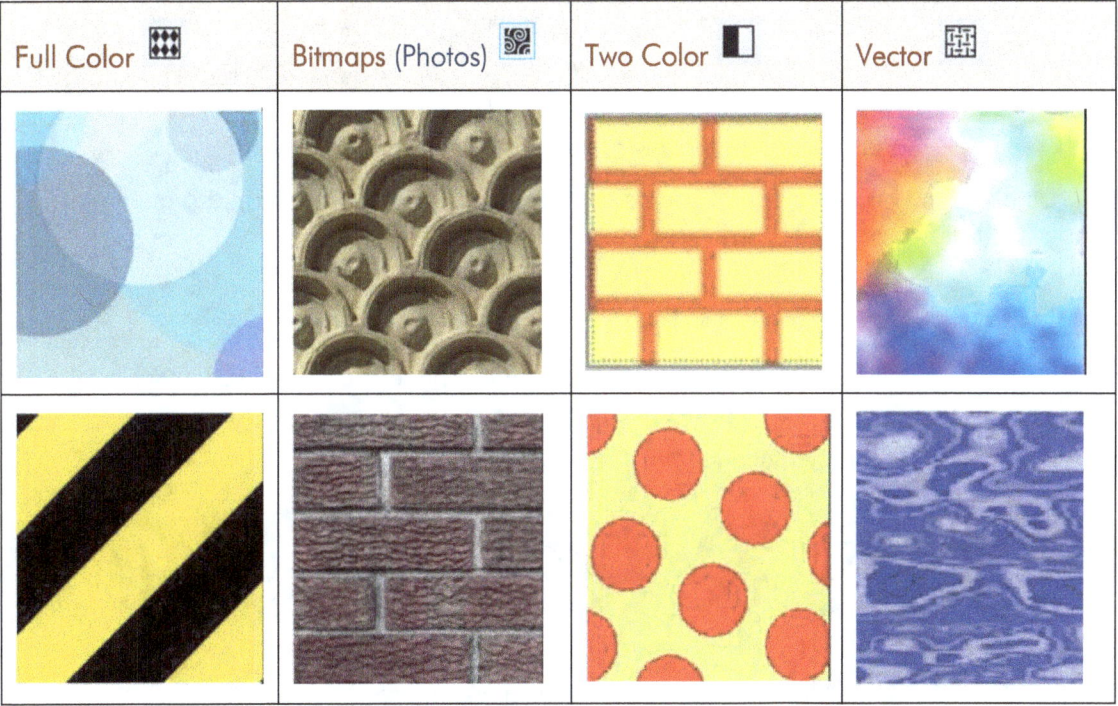

> In the case of the Essentials and Student Edition, the number of prefabricated filling patterns is unfortunately greatly reduced. Some fill patterns are incorrectly sorted, e.g., "Apples" in full colors instead of bitmaps, so look at all fillings from time to time.

14.1 Full Color Fillings

Here you'll find a collection of various fillings.

Here you find graphic work from designers, e.g., color stripes or filled circles.

Assign a full-color filling:

Mark the object to fill and then the interactive fill tool-vector or bitmap fill:

Choose a category on left side and then click a pattern on the scroll list.

14.2 BITMAP-PATTERN FILLINGS

Here you will find fillings from real photos, e.g., from above photographed metal sheet or evergreen, too bad, with earlier versions there was a lot more choice, e.g., Coffee beans, cherries photographed from above, etc.

- With Bitmap Pattern Fills, experts from real photos can be used.
  - Bitmap, the file extension bmp, was used in early PC times by Windows for the Windows wallpaper images.
  - Thus, it is clear that we have to do it here with a pixel-filling so composed of points - with all the drawbacks, such as jagged edges.

bmp

Assign bitmap filling:
- Select another rectangle and apply a bitmap fill. As with the full-color pattern fill, just choose a fill from the preview window.
  - Note that you can then adjust the fill size and rotation on the lever handles.

Some are clippings of real photos and some are graphic work from designers, or both combined.

14.3 TWO-COLOR FILLING

- The fill pattern "Two-colors" is a painted pattern of only two colors in contrast to the colorful full-color fills.
  - The preference for two color is black and white, but you can choose other colors with the color buttons.

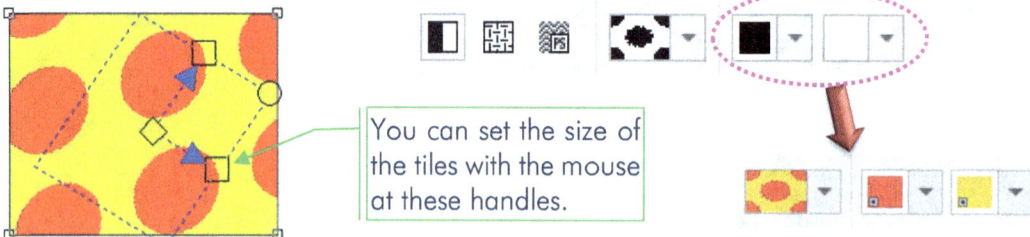

You can set the size of the tiles with the mouse at these handles.

14.4 TEXTURE FILL – THE CORELDRAW FILLINGS

These fillings drawn by graphic artists are the specialty of CorelDraw. Many of the Corel designed colored vector pattern fillings are very nice e.g., for a book title page.

- Mark a new rectangle, switch to the Texture Fillings, now you can choose a filling type in the Property bar:

Choose a collection here.

And then a filling type here.

More setting options in the filling menu:

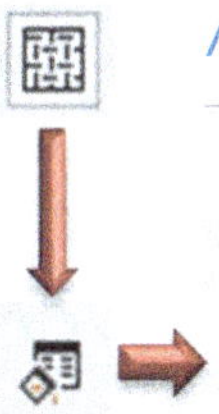

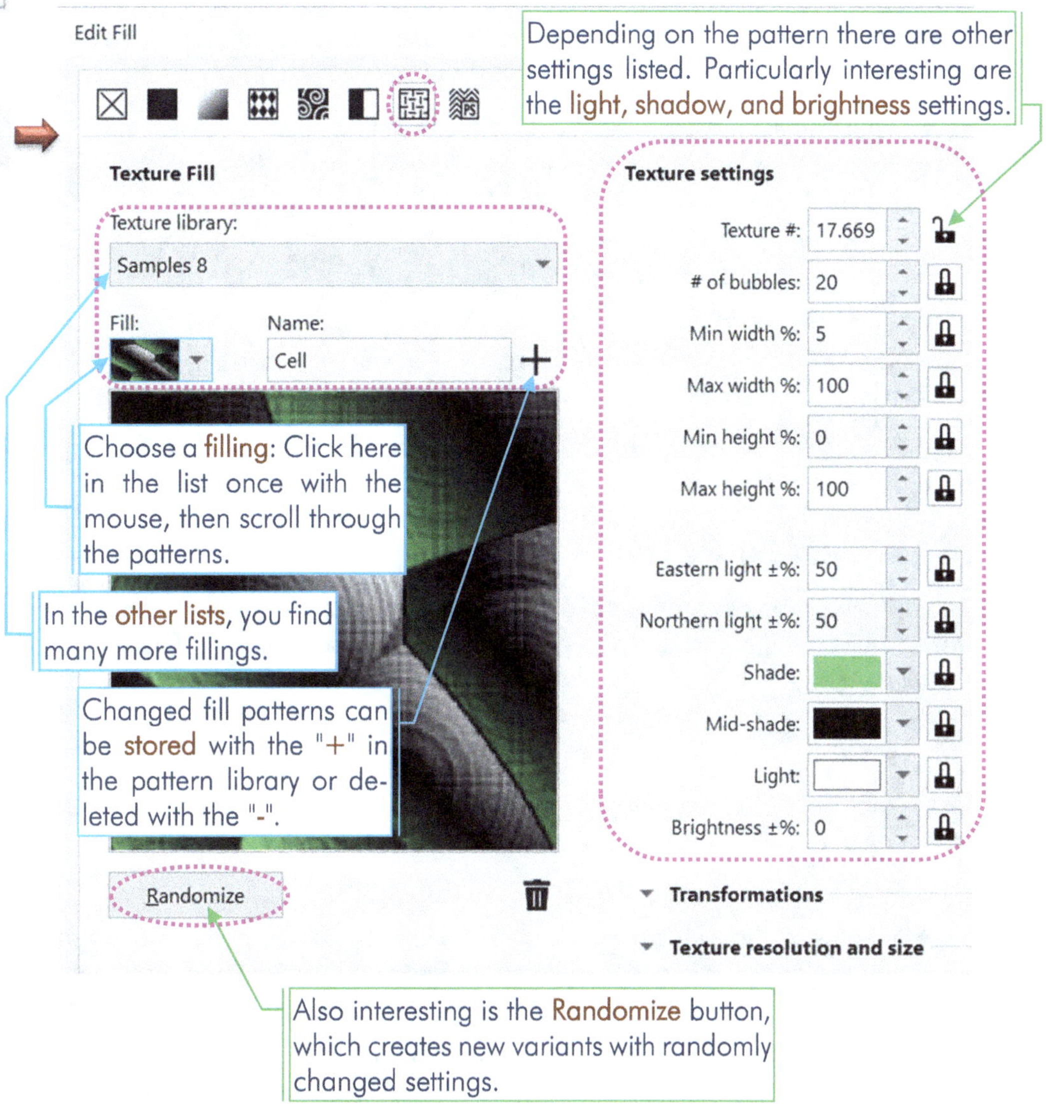

Depending on the pattern there are other settings listed. Particularly interesting are the light, shadow, and brightness settings.

Choose a filling: Click here in the list once with the mouse, then scroll through the patterns.

In the other lists, you find many more fillings.

Changed fill patterns can be stored with the "+" in the pattern library or deleted with the "-".

Also interesting is the Randomize button, which creates new variants with randomly changed settings.

- Texture library: even more fill patterns are hidden here.
- Texture # and # of bubbles: click and try different variations of actual patterns, with more or fewer bubbles you have many possibilities for new filling patterns.
- Modified fill patterns can be saved in the fill pattern library with the "+", the current pattern is deleted with the recycle bin icon.

14.5 Postscript Patterns

Postscript is a standardized printer language developed in early 1980s from Adobe. The feature is that the print result is same between home office printer and print shop if both use postscript. Today most PDF formats, from Adobe, too, use it for same result.

> Choose the postscript patterns. You'll find some fillings consume less computing power. Look at the fill pattern; unfortunately, only a few are colored.

14.6 THE TILE SIZE

The pattern image is usually smaller than the object used to populate it. Therefore, the filling is made up of multiple images (tiles).

Tile

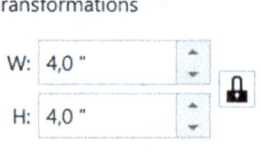

- With the bitmap and vector filling you can specify size with the mouse at the handles or in the menu by Transformations, but not with the Postscript fillings.
  - ↳ If the lock is closed, both dimensions are changed at the same time.
- The option "Transform with object" causes the filling to be scaled in case of subsequent size changes.

14.7 MAKE A NEW PATTERN FILL

Bitmap fillings are from real photos. So, you can set each photo or an area from a photo or graphic as a new pattern fill, e.g., photos from the internet. In the filling menu by bitmap pattern fill you find these symbols:

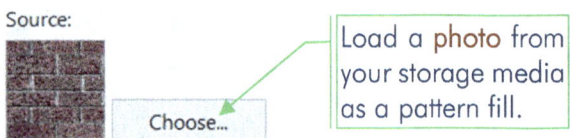

- If you only want to save a section of a photo as a fill pattern: open in Photo-Paint, save under a different name, and crop to the desired section.
  - ↳ With Object/Create/Pattern Fill you can mark an area of your actual drawing and can set it as a new pattern fill, also in Photo-Paint.

14.8 COPY A FILLING

If you want to re-record the filling of an object to assign it to another object, that comes with the pipette. The application is done simply, bearing in mind the selection menu:

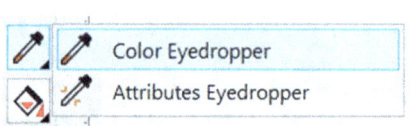

- With the Color Eyedropper you can pick up a color, but not a filling, and insert it into another object.
- A filling pattern can be picked up with the Attributes Eyedropper; hold the mouse button on the Color Eyedropper symbol and hold down as the selection menu opens.
  - ↳ Then click on the desired filling, then this can be assigned to any number of other objects.
- Alternatively, you can use the command "Edit/Copy Properties From..." e.g., to copy the filling from one object to another:
  - ↳ Mark the target first, then choose the above command and click on the object with the filling to copy.

15. ClipArt and Shadow

15.1 Insert ClipArt or Photos

You can import clip art and photos from any media, such as the Corel DVD, if available, other clip art collections, from the internet or from the Corel online library.

To insert clipart or photo's you have following options:

- ♦ Photos already saved on your hard drive can be inserted into the current drawing

    - ↳ via **Windows Explorer**: drag into the drawing while holding down the mouse button,
    - ↳ with **Import** or
    - ↳ right-click on the photo/copy and paste into Corel.

- ♦ Also possible with the **Corel "Assets"** utility (Window/Dockers, formerly called Corel Connect), which also allows Corel content to be downloaded and imported online.

Exercise Photo or ClipArt from the internet:

- ➢ Start your usual **Internet browser**, enter a search term at the top, e.g., **animal** or **plane**, confirm with Return and switch to the tab Photos or Pictures.

- ➢ Click on the desired photo first, so that the photo is displayed instead of the preview image, then **right-click** on it, **copy**, switch to the CorelDRAW drawing and **right-click/paste**.

    - ↳ In the Internet browser, right-click on the photo and select Save Image As. If you want to save it on your hard disk, you can then **import** it into CorelDRAW or Photo-Paint.

15.2 The Corel Assets

Many objects (animals …) that can be inserted into new drawings which are available on the Corel website. You should, therefore, take a look at them, as you can save a lot of work if you can use a finished object.

- You can find them in the Assets at **Window/Dockers/Assets**, scroll the list, choose instead "All Content" a category, or if you want you can enter a search term there in the search magnifier, e.g., animal, dolphin etc.

Insert into the drawing:

- Inserting into the drawing is done as usual: **drag** into the drawing area with the left mouse button pressed or right-click on it and import or click on the image and select the Import symbol below left in Assets.

↳ For example, if you drag a clip art onto a previously selected rectangle, the photo will be inserted as a fill for this rectangle.

In addition, almost only a little content can be found on the **Home & Student Edition** online.

Notes on Corel Assets:[2]

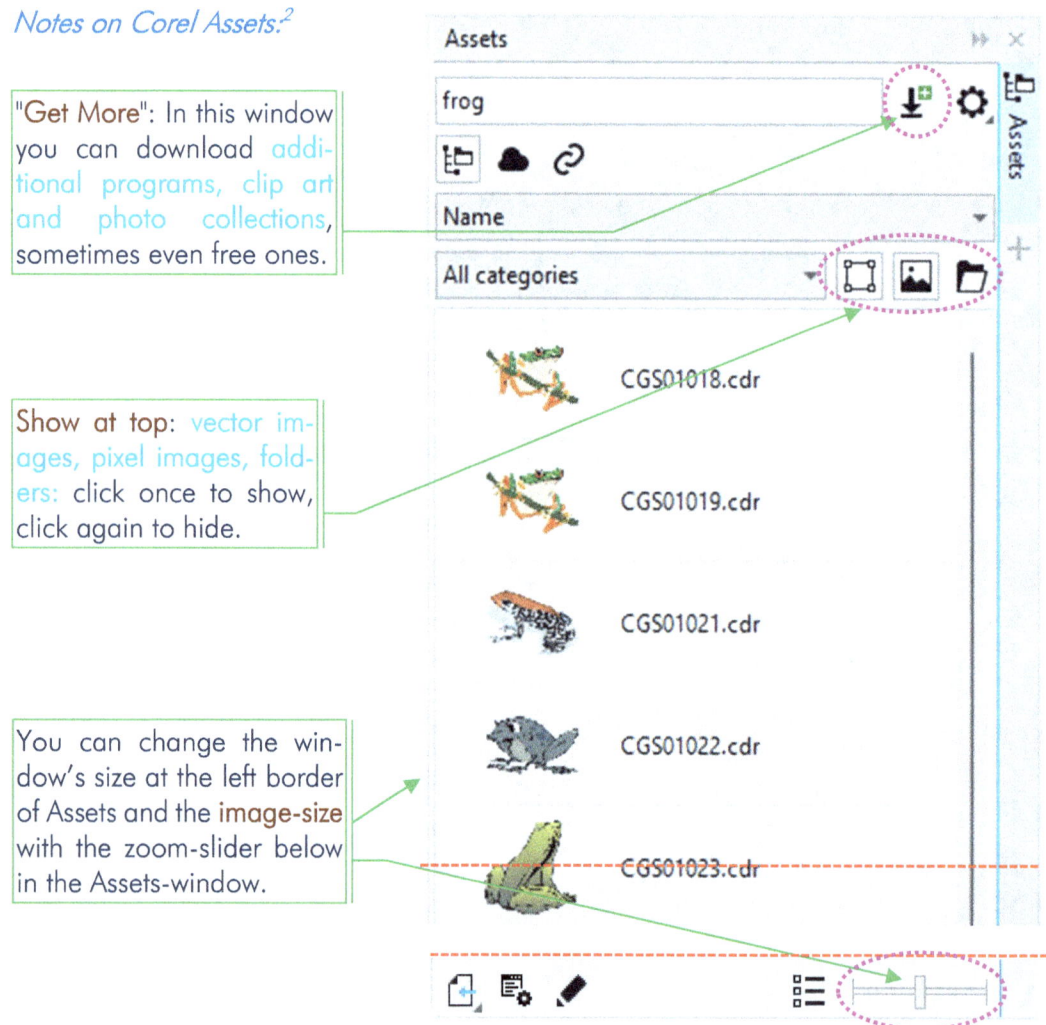

"Get More": In this window you can download *additional programs, clip art and photo collections*, sometimes even free ones.

Show at top: *vector images, pixel images, folders:* click once to show, click again to hide.

You can change the window's size at the left border of Assets and the *image-size* with the zoom-slider below in the Assets-window.

---

[2] Formerly called "Connect"

15.3 Exercise: Birthday Invitation

An exercise about inserting a clipart. With the countless finished clipart choices, it is necessary to draw only in the professional field.

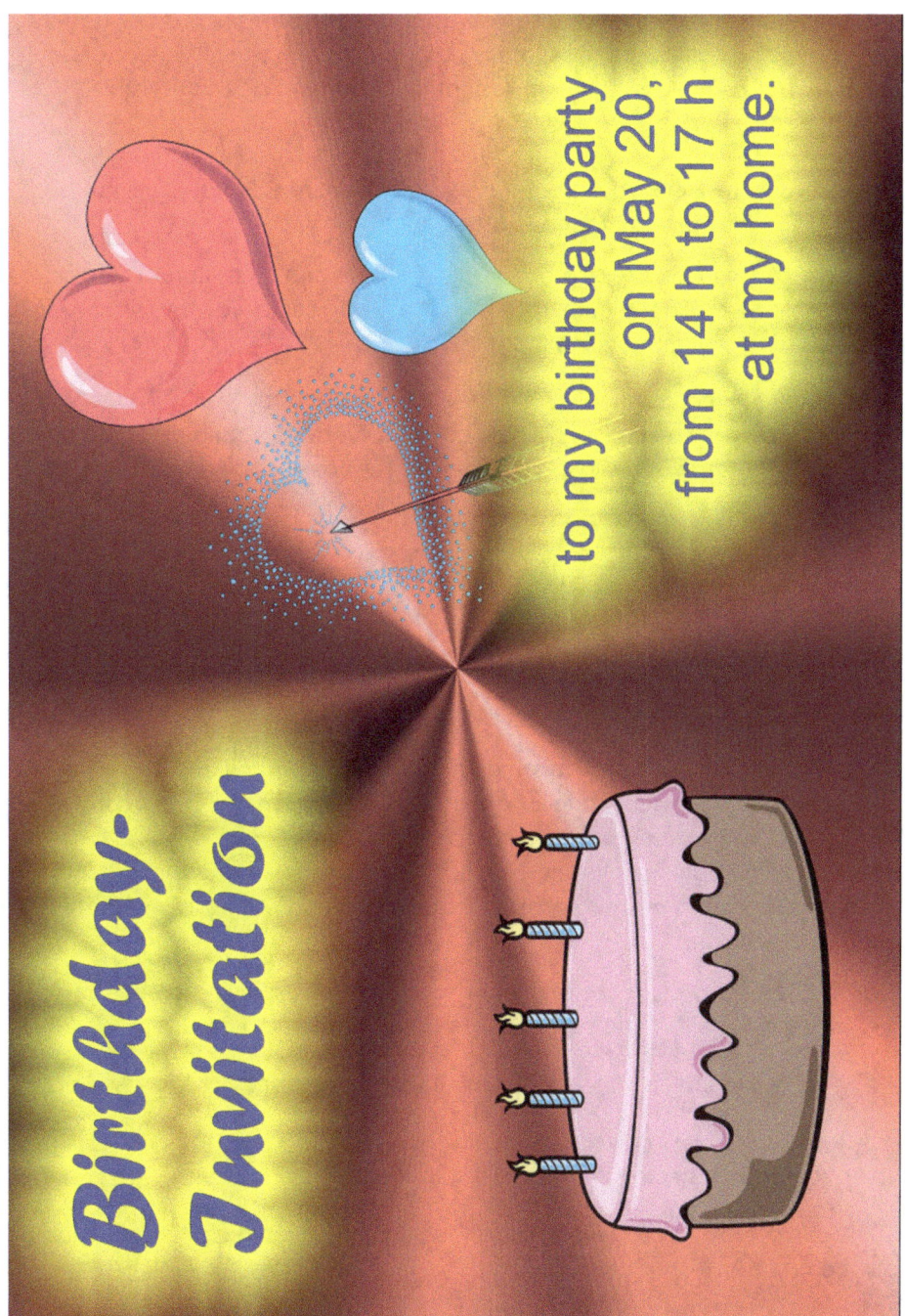

- ➢ New drawing with DIN A4 landscape.
- ➢ Search in your web browser for example "birthday cliparts",
- ➢ then click on the Photos tab, click on appropriate clip art to enlarge
- ➢ and right-click/copy and paste in Corel.

15.3.1 BACKGROUND FOR WHOLE PAGE

- ➢ You can set a colored background easily by drawing a rectangle the same size as the page, filling it and placing it back.
  - ✎ Here a conical gradient fill was created by himself: color gradient / edit / conical, then set many color points and select "repeat and mirror" as the arrangement so that no beginning or end is visible.

- ♦ If you draw the background first, you often accidentally get the background if you want to move an element.
  - ✎ This can be prevented as follows: Right mouse button on the background rectangle, then Lock. Unlock with same way with right mouse button on the object, then unlock.
- ♦ With the command Layout/Page Background by Layout/Page Background you can specify a single color as the background or load a photo by "Bitmap". But a color gradient filling is not possible there.
  - ✎ The "Print and Export Background" option is sometimes practical. If you disable this, you can use a background color to simulate a colored paper on the screen without printing this color.

15.3.2 SHADOW TOOL (NOT BY ESSENTIALS)

Unfortunately, this effect is missing in the Essentials Edition. Then use the "Transform" menu described in Chapter 10.3 and 19.1 to create a copy offset by 0.1 mm, for example, which goes on the far left at Position, and assign a different color to this copy, and a self-made shadow is ready. In this change menu, you can also move this shadow slightly instead of copying it in order to adjust the position.

Now the text follows. As we apply our first effect by assigning a shadow to it, the effect of this effort can be better seen against the background.

- ➢ Write the text as two text blocks, then arrange and set them separately as shown.
- ➢ Assign a matching color gradient to the text.

In the case of text, a deposited shadow is beautiful. Even a continuous shadow can be realized.

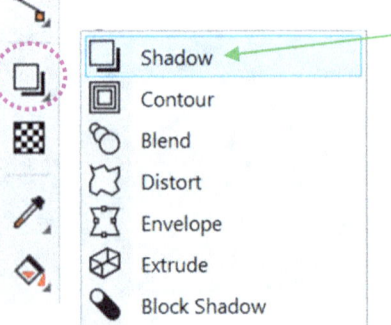

Open the selection menu for the effects and select the Shadow (Most of these effects are missing from Essentials).

- ➢ From the text beginning with the mouse button pressed, draw an arrow which shows the provisional shadow or, at the top of the property bar, a presetting, e.g., "Medium Glow".

Shadow with the mouse at a sample text:

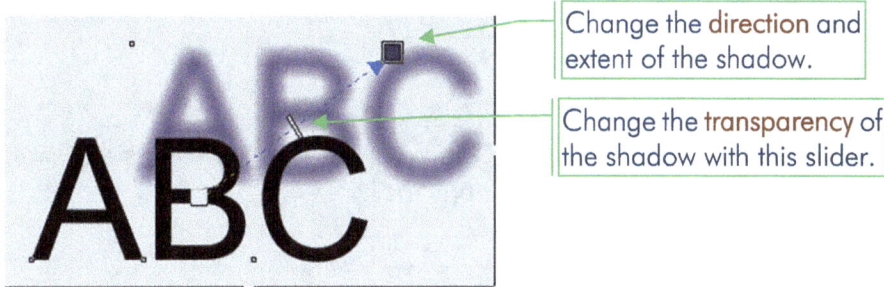

The Property bar for the drop shadow:

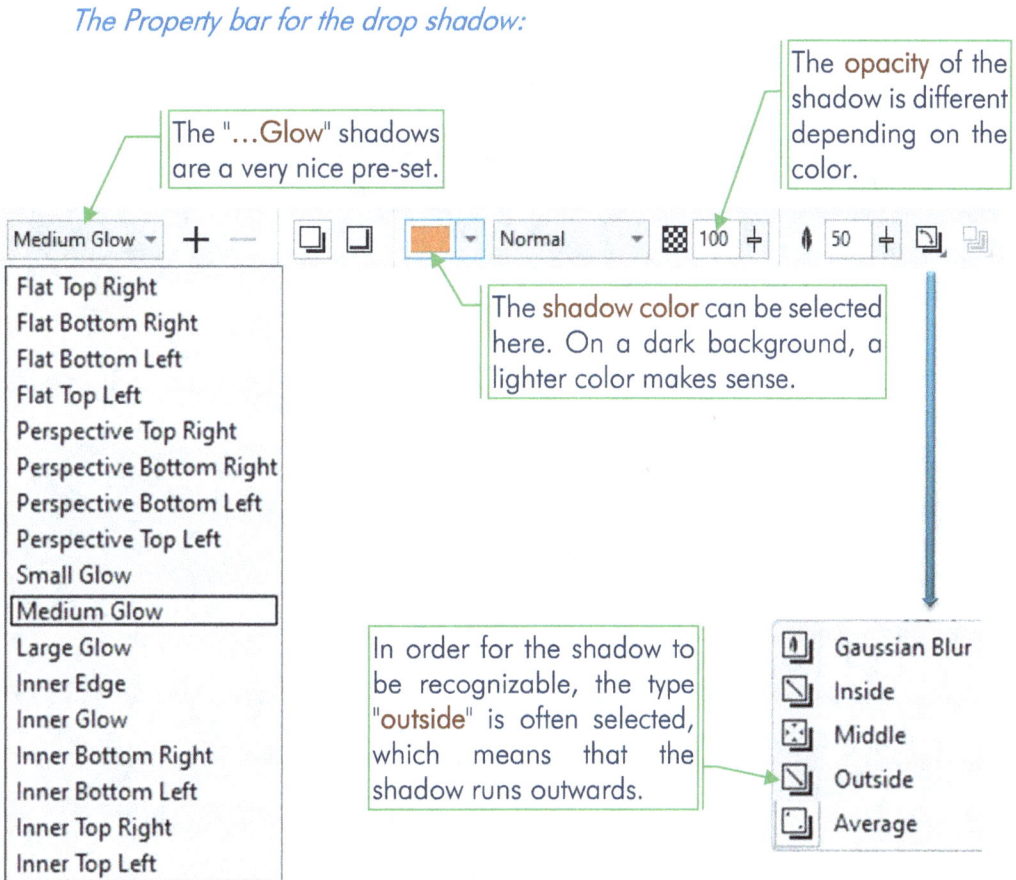

On a dark background, a lighter color makes sense and vice versa.

Notes: ....
....
....
....
....
....

15.4 Insert ClipArt

A small advertisement as an exercise:

- New drawing with half letter size.
- Import a matching ClipArt, e.g., search in the web "wine glass drawing", adjust the size and move to the right position.

Set the grid and use guidelines as edge markings. This helps to set the text to correct positions.

★ Draw an ellipse similar to the red dotted, then put it behind the clip art. (property bar).
★ Assign a white filling to the ellipse and set it slightly transparent, approx. 20%. Thus, the background is hidden something.

A shadow is nice for text most of the time. We have also added a shadow to the headline. Make sure the two shadows look much the same.

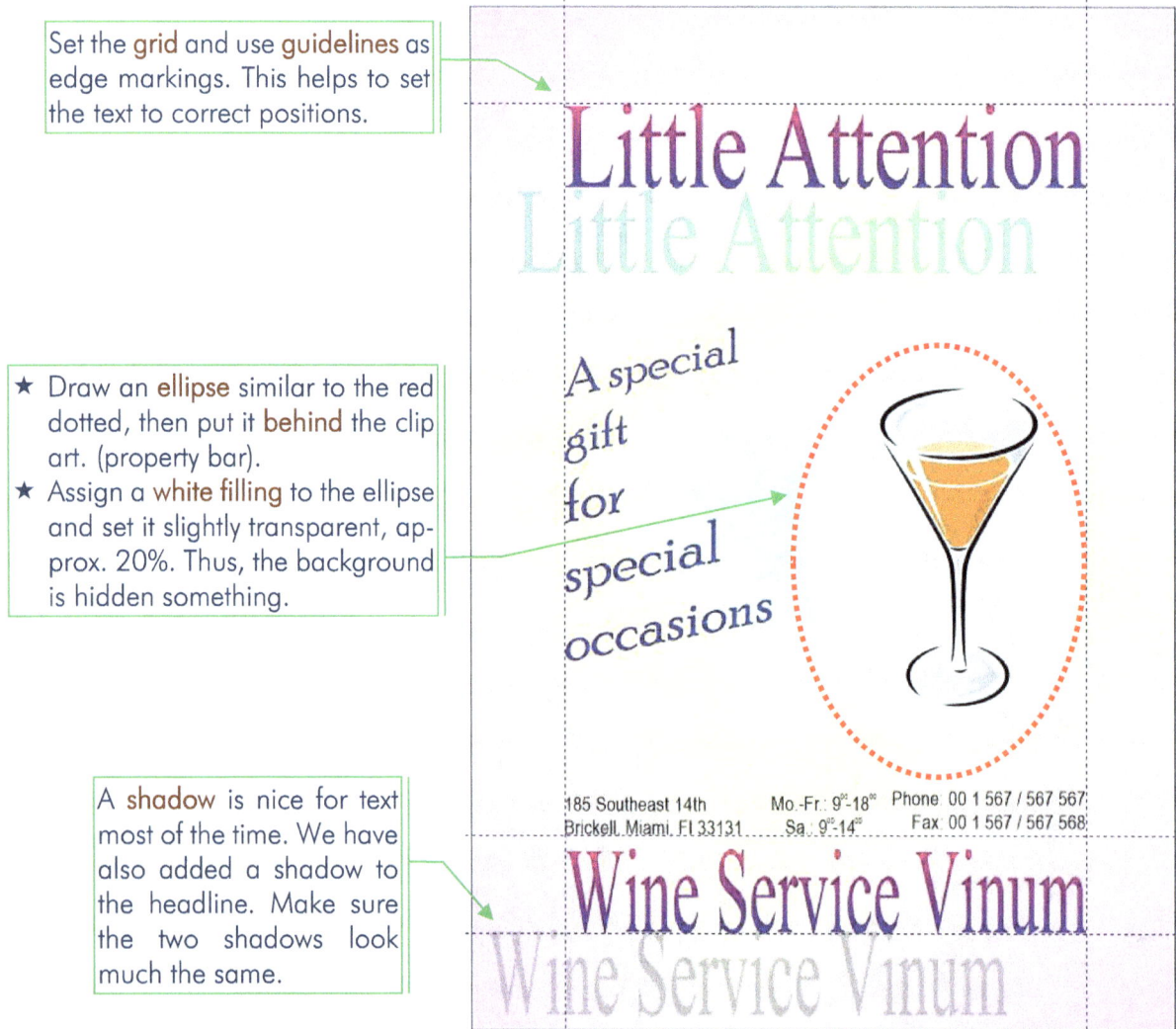

If the champagne glass has a background to be removed:

- If you use a clip art: Ungroup, then delete unwanted items, then group them again.
- For photos: Draw an ellipse over it as desired, select effect lens, lighten by e.g., 5% and "Fixed", then you can move this image section, delete the original image, we have created a section in ellipse size.
- Finally fill the text, arrange it and fill it in with color.
- As the background, draw a rectangle as large as the page and fill it. Here a radial color sequence was assigned.

16. Interactive Menus

We discussed the interactive filling starting on page 71, but now we want to go into detail about the specialty of this type of interactive filling.

Interactive means that you can change settings directly with the mouse on the object instead of in a menu e.g., the direction of a color flow fill.

With the mouse, however, only the most important values can be set, also in the property bar, all other settings can be found in the respective menus.

16.1 Interactive Fill Pattern

In the case of the interactive filling, all the previously described can be set in the property bar. Fillings can thus be easily assigned. Here are some options.

➢ Draw a rectangle in a new drawing and select the Interactive Fill tool.

➢ Hold the mouse button while drawing and you set the start and end points and the direction of the color gradient filling.

➢ At last, you can define the start and end color: Click on the boxes at the beginning and the end of the arrow and select one color at a time.

  ✎ You can choose colors either from the property bar, from the "Node Color" drop-down menu, or simply from the color palette.

Adjust with the mouse:

You can also use the mouse to determine the starting and ending colors by clicking on a box of the color gradient arrow and clicking a color from the color palette.

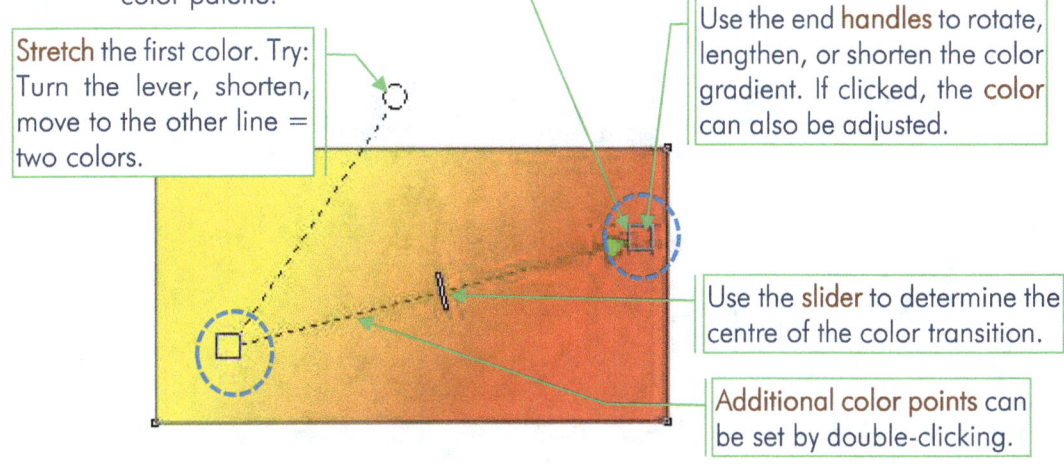

Stretch the first color. Try: Turn the lever, shorten, move to the other line = two colors.

Use the end handles to rotate, lengthen, or shorten the color gradient. If clicked, the color can also be adjusted.

Use the slider to determine the centre of the color transition.

Additional color points can be set by double-clicking.

Now, these symbols appear in the property bar:

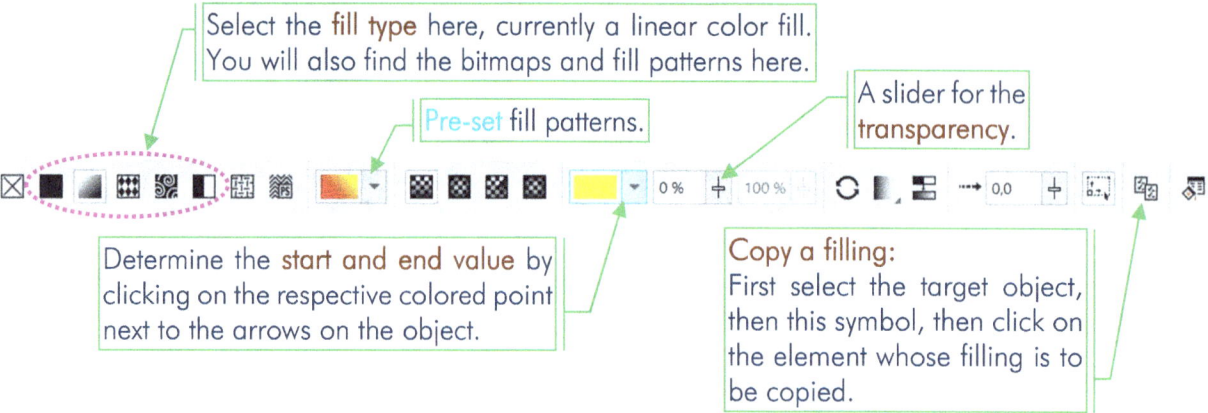

Select the fill type here, currently a linear color fill. You will also find the bitmaps and fill patterns here.

Pre-set fill patterns.

A slider for the transparency.

Determine the start and end value by clicking on the respective colored point next to the arrows on the object.

Copy a filling:
First select the target object, then this symbol, then click on the element whose filling is to be copied.

> You can set the fill in the property bar or with the mouse on the object. Depending on the selected fill, other symbols are available that you already know from the previous chapters.

16.2 INTERACTIVE MESH FILL (NOT BY ESSENTIALS)

In this fill method, a mesh grid is placed in the selected object. Then a color can be drawn into each area. A color carpet is created.

➤ Select or draw a new rectangle, then hold down the left mouse button on the interactive fill symbol until the selection menu appears and change it to the mesh fill.

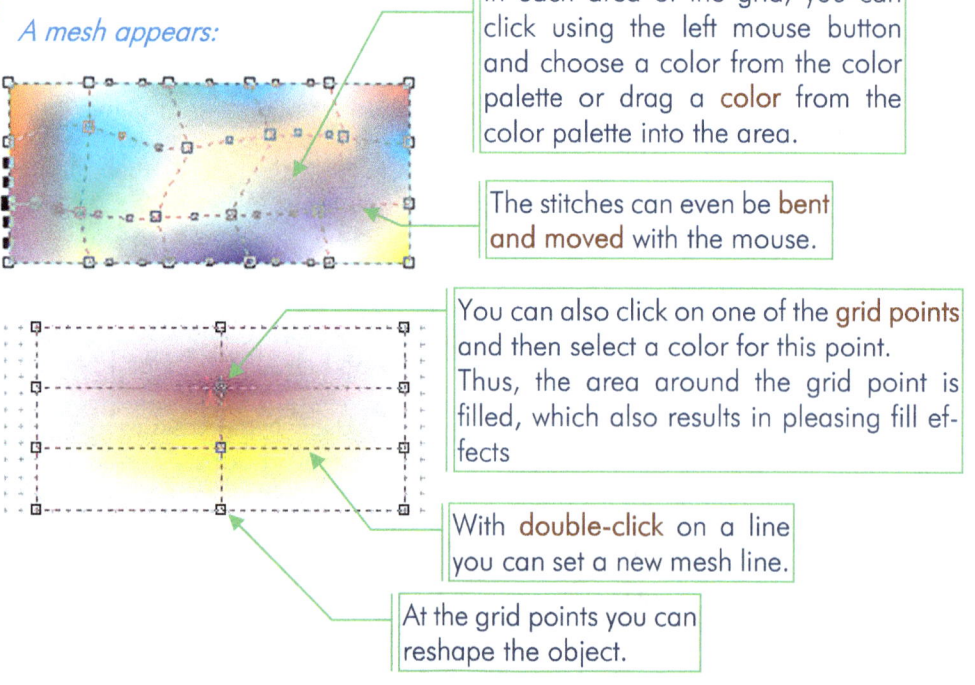

A mesh appears:

In each area of the grid, you can click using the left mouse button and choose a color from the color palette or drag a color from the color palette into the area.

The stitches can even be bent and moved with the mouse.

You can also click on one of the grid points and then select a color for this point. Thus, the area around the grid point is filled, which also results in pleasing fill effects

With double-click on a line you can set a new mesh line.

At the grid points you can reshape the object.

The following setting options appear in the Property Bar:

Here you can set more or fewer grid lines.

Choose the color of the selected mesh.

16.3 Interactive Transparency (not by Essentials)

In the Toolbox on left side, you'll find the symbol for the transparency, so that the underlying objects glimmer through.

➢ Draw a new **rectangle**, fill with a color.

➢ Then draw an **ellipse** within this rectangle and assign it a fill color, too.

➢ Then choose the **Transparency tool** and either use the **mouse** to drag a transparency arrow within the ellipse or set the transparency in the **Property bar**.

In the case of transparency, fillings can also be selected as a mask:

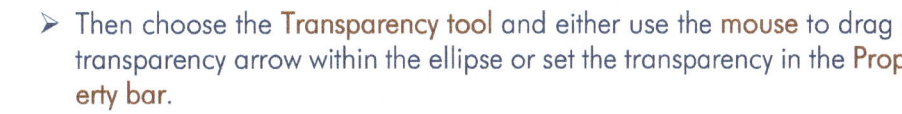

No Transparency.

A **transparency slider** controls the transparency.

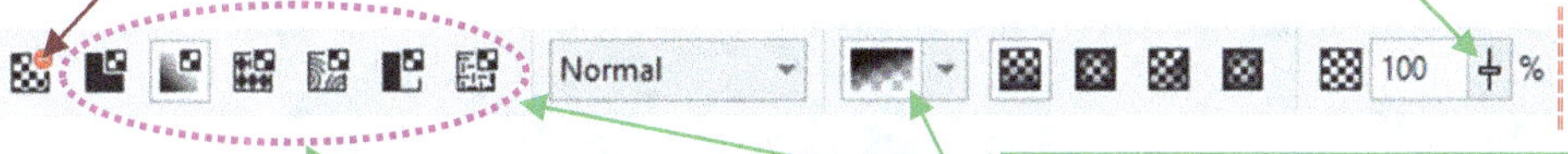

As with the fillings, **patterns** can be selected, but these are now translucent (see the following example with the wall filling).

Similar to color patterns, **uniform, fountain, vector, bitmap, bi-color transparency** can be selected, but now it is not a color fill, but a transparency.

Right side of property bar:

Edit Transparency.

With "**freeze**" the object can be moved, the background is retained.

Transparency with the mouse:

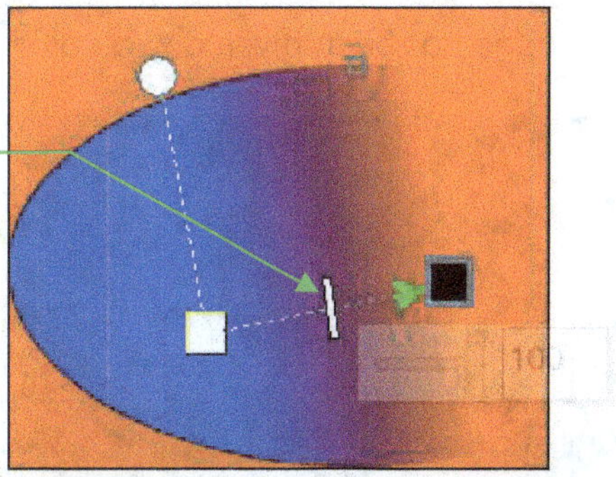

The **slider** for 50% transparency, adjust at the handles the size and angle.

Transparency with the two-color pattern "Wall":

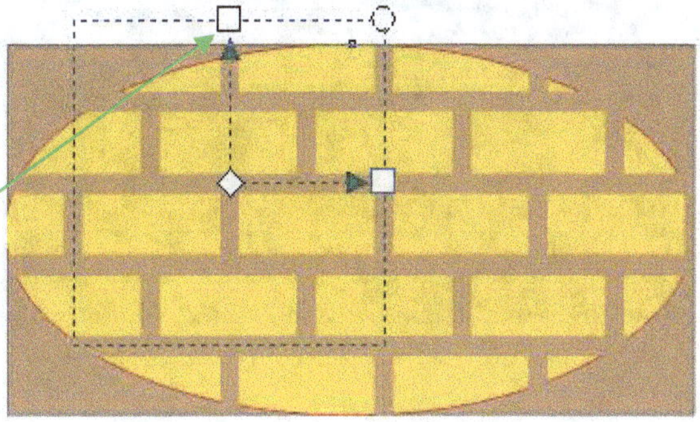

The **pattern size** and direction can be set on the handles of the arrows.

16.4 Inserting Photos

This **interactive transparency** is particularly excellent when the effects are used to make a photo more and more dynamic.

This is what we try to do with a new exercise. On page 89, you have already inserted clipart. Likewise, you can insert photos same way.

> ➢ **New exercise**, looking for two photos on the web: **shark** and **flower meadow**, click on each and let it display in normal size, right mouse button on / copy, paste in the Corel, about the same size as the sheet of paper set, possibly margins of one photo cut something.

> ➢ Then use the **transparency tool** to drag a temporary transparency arrow:

Specify the **transparency** by an arrow.

You can then move the **transparency arrow** as you like, or change its length at the ends, making the transition wider or sharper.

The **slider** in the centre applies to the centre of transparency (50% transmittance).

> ➢ Then try the other **transparency settings** in the **property bar** such as Regular or Radial or Pattern, instead of linear transparency. Here, the flower image has been given a two-color transparency:

Try to **invert** the two-color-transparency (only by two-color transparency).

Fourth Part

Curve Editing, Text Options and Paragraph Text

*Something looks different?
Use Window-Workspace-Default
(not by Essentials Edition)*

17. Curve Editing

Now to the best of CorelDRAW: Self drawing!

- ♦ The moon, speakers, stars and figures in the following exercise we draw manual, and since this does not work out perfectly right away, we use the Shape Tool to reshape.
  - ↘ With this tool, we can change the endpoints of lines or the points at which a curve changes direction.

For the Christmas tree exercise on page 80, you have already applied the Form tool, but now we explore its full capabilities.

17.1 Exercise: Party

This exercise is ideal for practicing copying with the mouse, including grouping, multiple fillings, and especially curves.

For the stars, the moon and the figures, the curve processing is necessary, an excellent function with which even difficult curves can be adapted bit by bit.

The background is a color gradient fill. To fill a page, a normal rectangle is drawn across the entire page. Then the rectangle obscures all other objects and has to be set backwards. So that we do not inadvertently move this while drawing, either fix it or draw it last.

Preparations:

- New file, DIN A5 or letter landscape, grid every 5 mm.
- A horizontal **guide line** for the floor so that all objects can be arranged at the same height.

The speaker:

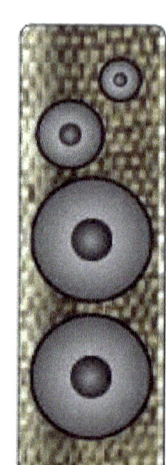

- Draw a rectangle as a speaker cabinet:
  - ★ Make it wide enough that in the middle is a grid row, so that the individual loudspeaker chassis can be drawn easily in the middle.
- Draw a **chassis** as a circle with a thick, different colored line:
  - ✎ Start in the middle of the chassis with the first point, hold [Ctrl] and [Shift] = Circle around the first point.
- Assign a **radial color gradient** fill, then copy the first circle in the middle and reduce it:
  - ✎ Hold the circle at a corner touch point, resize it while holding down [Shift] and click the **right mouse button** for copying.
  - ★ Switch off the line for this small inner circle.
- **Group on chassis**, then you can copy it easily and modify the size matching your imaginations.
- When a loudspeaker is ready, assign the fill to the enclosure and group it completely. Do not redo the second speaker - just copy it.

17.2 THE STARS – MOVE THE TURN POINTS

1. Draw a **star**: Deactivate grid, click start and end point once, otherwise double-click.
2. Now use the **Shape Tool** to move the corner points until the star looks halfway like a star (this can also be done with the Pick Tool).

- Fill the star, then copy the star several times, and rotate or resize each copy to vary their appearance.

This is a good exercise. But later you can use more easy stars from symbol fonts (see p. 68), or draw it with the **Polygon Tool**, or use the polyline (then only double-click first and last point, otherwise single click).

17.3 The Moon - Circle Segments

To draw the moon, we cut circular segments out of two circles and then connect them to one element to fill the moon.

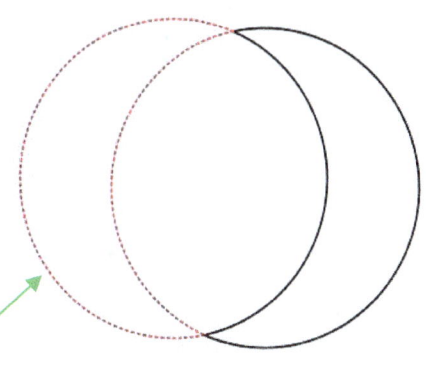

➢ Draw **one circle** (with pressed [Ctrl]-button) and copy it slightly offset:

Now these red marked circle parts have to be **cut off**.

➢ When the **Shape Tool** is selected, click a circle. At the top of the circle, a small dot appears (not the eight handle points on the outside!).

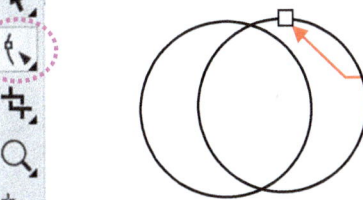

Open the circle at this small point a little and look at the line that remains. Just try and then move the line accordingly.

[Alt]-Y

Now temporarily disable "**Align to Grid**" to allow the circular segments to meet.

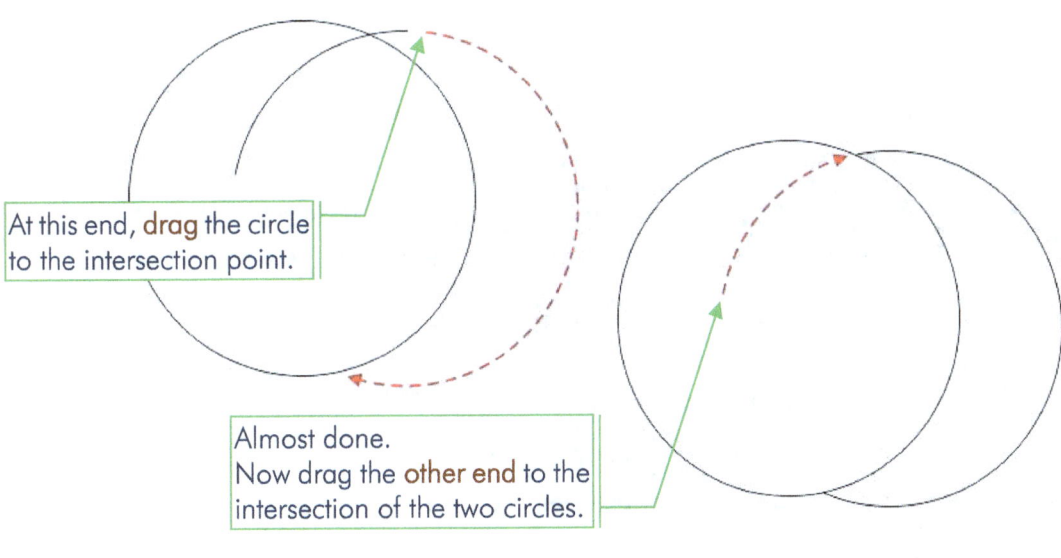

At this end, **drag the circle** to the intersection point.

Almost done.
Now drag the **other end** to the intersection of the two circles.

Cake piece or bow:

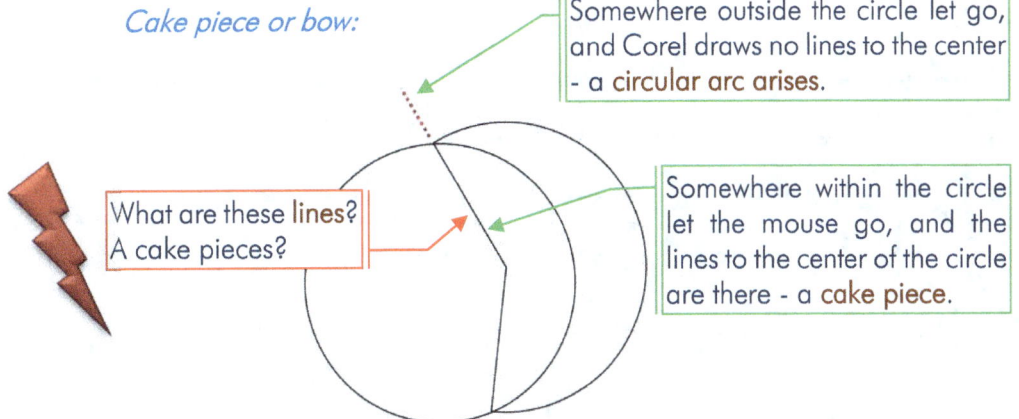

Somewhere outside the circle let go, and Corel draws no lines to the center - a **circular arc** arises.

What are these lines? A cake pieces?

Somewhere within the circle let the mouse go, and the lines to the center of the circle are there - a **cake piece**.

> No unnecessary thoughts needed to see which part is preserved. Open something, then see in which direction it goes.

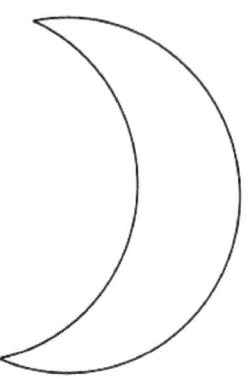

➢ Now transform the second circle to the arc and the moon is finished.

Well, that was once a very useful drawing function.

17.4 COMBINE TO FILL

Filling is usually not yet possible, because for Corel there are only two circular arcs, which have nothing to do with each other. So, we must tell Corel that this is a connected figure, a moon:

➢ Mark both arcs and combine them.

↳ This can be done with a symbol in the property bar, as soon as several objects are selected, in the menu with Object/Combine or with Shortcut [Ctrl]-L.

[Ctrl]-L

For marking:

- If you press [Shift], you can select with the pick tool several objects by clicking on them.
  ↳ As long as you press the [Shift] key, you can also delete a marking.
  ↳ Note the message in the status bar at the bottom of the Corel window:
  "2 Objects Selected on Layer 1".

The difference between Group and Combine:

- Group summarizes objects to an element.
- Combine if you want to fill between two objects.

Notes: ....
....
....
....
....
....
....

17.5 Closing of the Figure

In most situations, it is still not enough to fill the moon.

> ➢ Try it by clicking on a color of the color palette with the right mouse button.

Filling is not yet possible because the endpoints of the two arcs are not yet exactly met. Zoom in on the endpoints and you will see it in your drawing.

There we have the evil. But this can be corrected with the Shape Tool.

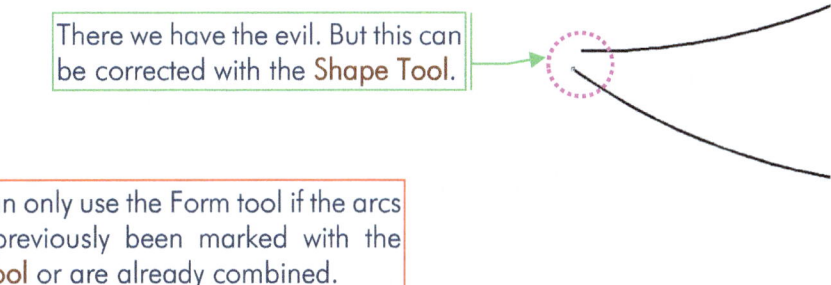

You can only use the Form tool if the arcs have previously been marked with the Pick Tool or are already combined.

Use the Shape Tool to draw a marker frame so large that both endpoints of the arcs are completely included.

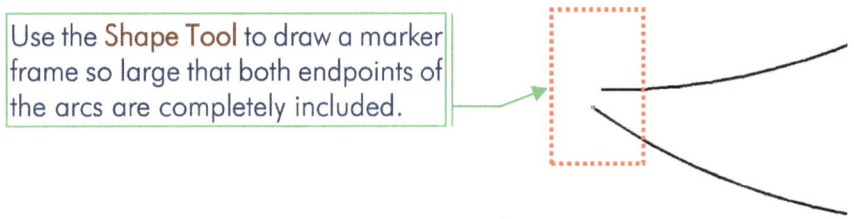

Now the necessary commands appear in the Property Bar:

If the endpoints of both curves are not touching, this easy-to-recognize symbol "Join two nodes" (nodes = turn points) is highlighted.

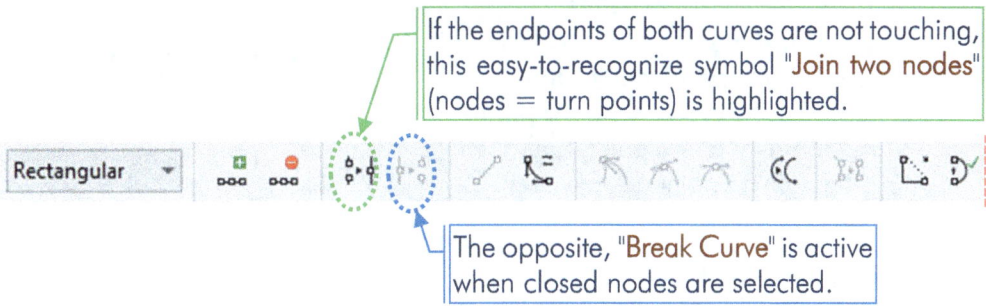

The opposite, "Break Curve" is active when closed nodes are selected.

Is it time to fill the moon? If not, only these two sources of error can be considered:

- The arcs are not yet combined or inadvertently grouped instead.

- The endpoints are not closed. Check with a strong zoom, and if necessary, repeat the procedure as described above.

17.6 Add Turn Points for the Nose

The moon looks quite nice, but can be even more beautiful. We'll add a big nose.

Features of the Shape Tool:

All possible objects can be added or changed at any time. Even very difficult bodies can be drawn piece by piece.

> A turning point is already quite present in the middle. Click on this point and choose Cusp Node in the property bar, so that we get sharp corners and no round curves.

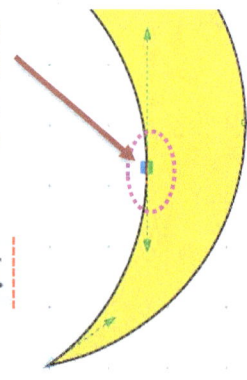

 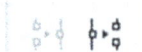  

> We will **add a point** a little more here with the Shape Tool.
>> The fastest method is to add a new point by double-clicking on the curve line. This also immediately switch to a Cusp Node point.
>> Other method: use the Shape Tool to set a provisional point, then press the + in the property bar or on the keyboard for a new point. Only then is the turning point actually set.

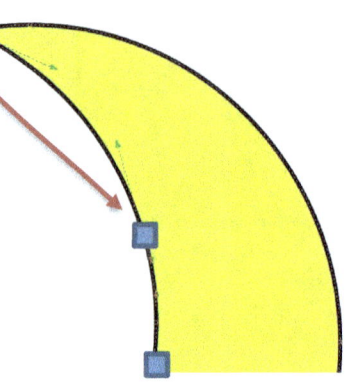

> Now you can use the mouse to draw the curve between the two new turning points and pull it out.
>> Do not touch the two levers, since it is then double work, but pull out the curve in the middle between the two turning points.

First bulge in the **middle**, then adjust the nose more appropriately at these arrows (levers, tangents).

Lever for fine adjustment. Each turning point has two arrows for the two directions.

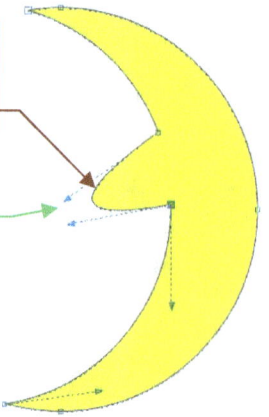

A nose is formed. More about the levers in the next chapter. Under the nose, you could just as well add a mouth.

17.7 THE FIGURES – ADAPT THEIR SHAPE

Also, line figures cannot be filled as long as there is not a closed line around.

Proceed as follows:

- Draw approximately the bodies.
  - With polylines or normal line and double-click.
- As with the stars, use the Shape Tool to make the figures close enough to correct.
- Try, if you can, to fill the figures.
  - If not, as by the moon, close the turning points with the Shape Tool until filling is possible.
- Only when the bodies are already filled, then we will supplement the arms:

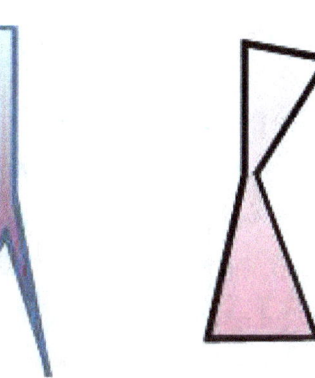

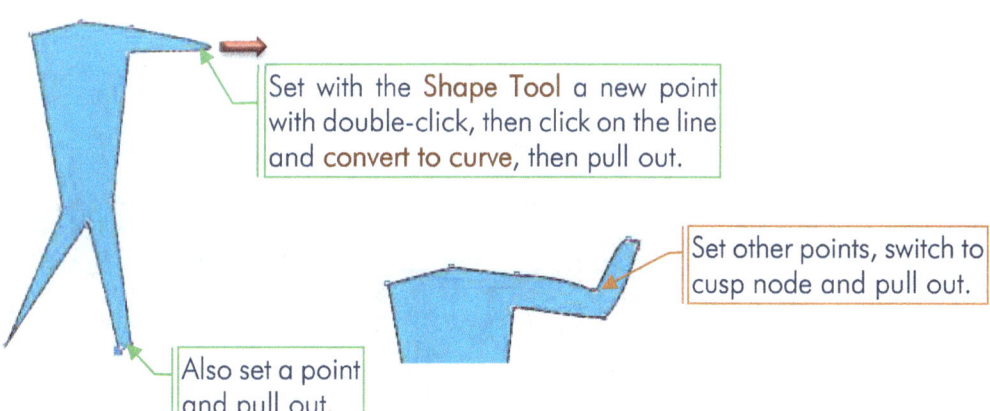

Set with the Shape Tool a new point with double-click, then click on the line and convert to curve, then pull out.

Set other points, switch to cusp node and pull out.

Also set a point and pull out.

- Hands and heads (ellipses) at high zoom:

Draw with Freehand Tool, then push and put backwards.

Draw with Freehand Tool, then push to head and put in front.

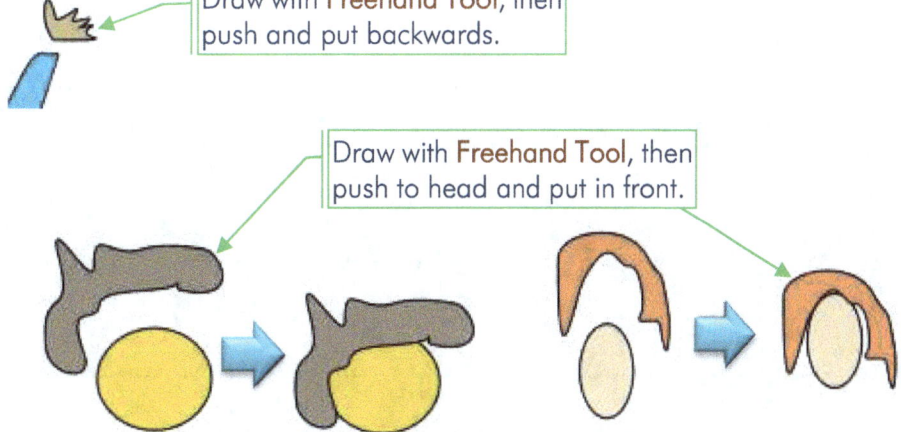

➢ We also draw the feet very simply with the **Freehand Tool**:

 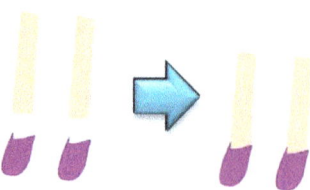

➢ With **high zoom** you can draw the eyes, mouth and nose with the tools you know (ellipses, freehand, curve lines) if you want.

  ✎ How eyes, noses and mouths can be drawn better follows in the next chapter step by step. Those who want can return to this drawing later to replace the eyes, mouth and nose with the later lessons.

➢ At the end, **group** each figure to make it an element, and the arrangement cannot be accidentally destroyed.

As an alternative, you could use characters from a symbolic font, or search for suitable clipart from the Corel clipart database or from the Internet.

Also, symbols and clipart can be changed with the **shape tool**. Sometimes necessary to ungroup them before redrawing is possible.

Notes:

18. THE SNAKE – CURVES TOTAL

Compared to the snake, all the previous practice was only a small pre-exercise. But no fear, it will not be much more difficult; however, you will now realize how powerful the Shape Tool is.

➢ New drawing, size first 100 mm wide, 210 mm height.
  ★ Set the Grid every 5 mm and activate align on grid and set guidelines as border lines by 10, 90 vertically and 10, 150 horizontally.

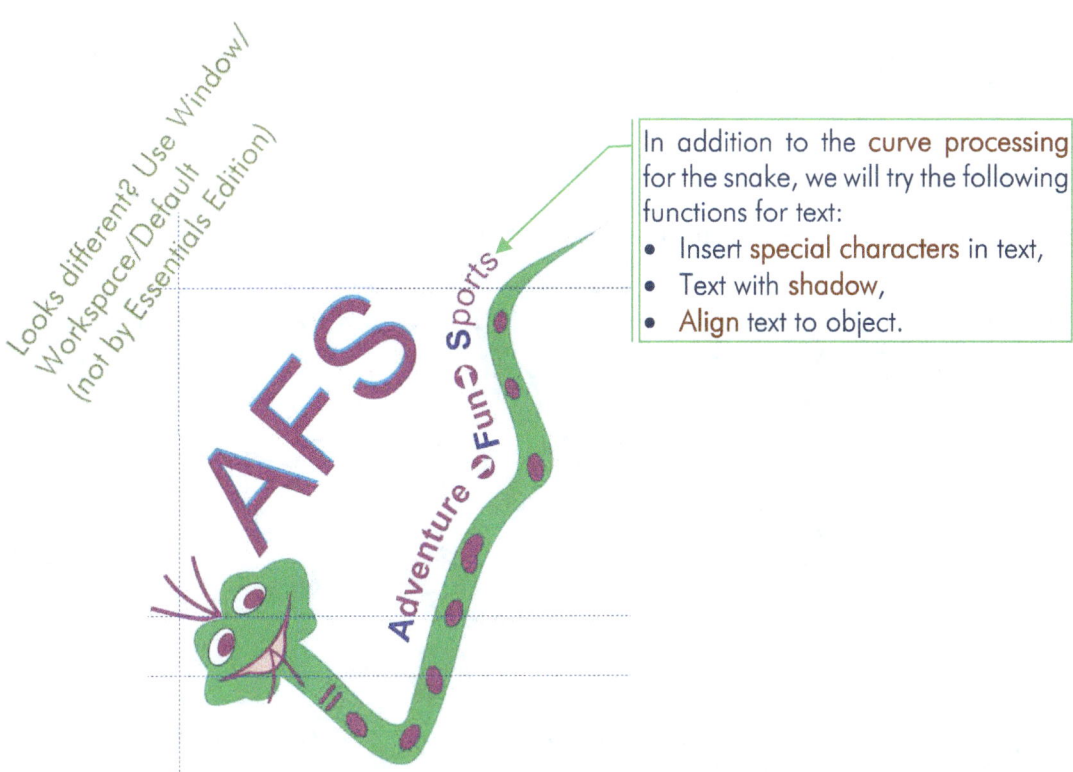

In addition to the curve processing for the snake, we will try the following functions for text:
- Insert special characters in text,
- Text with shadow,
- Align text to object.

Adventure ▶ Fun ▶ Sports Ltd.
321 Pearl Street
New York, New York, 10038 USA
Phone +1-123-123-4566
Fax: +1-123-123-4566-50

18.1 First Preliminary Exercise

So that it is not too difficult, we begin with only one curve.

- Draw a straight line in the side edge, approx. 5 cm long. [F5]

- Click with the **Shape Tool** in the middle of the line, to set a provisional point. [F10]
- Because we have selected a line, the **Convert to Curve button** is active. Click it to make a curve out of the line:

Switch to curve, left switch to line.

For turning points: cusp, smooth, symmetric.

Do not hold the line by the levers, but rather in the middle and bend them to a **curve**.

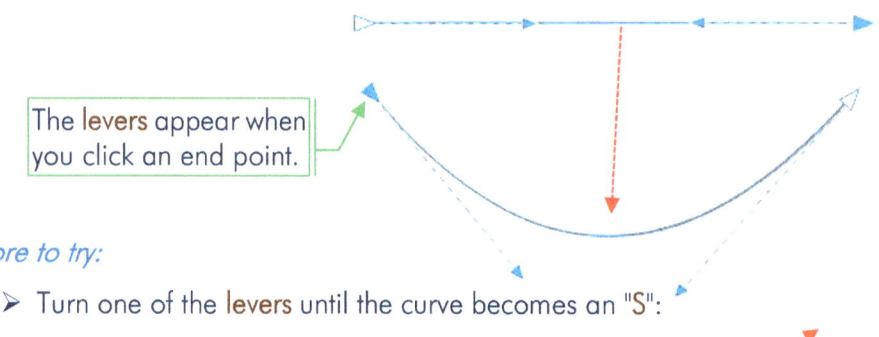

The **levers** appear when you click an end point.

More to try:

- Turn one of the **levers** until the curve becomes an "S":

- **Move** an initial point of the curve.

- Turn one of the **levers** and observe the effect.

- Pull a lever all the way out - the curve bulges - and then very small - the curve is easy to bounce.

Levers are tangents! About the levers:

♦ **Long levers** complicate the handling in practice.

♦ In addition, you can see that two curves (S) can be made from one stretch.

Levers

♦ We therefore need only very few turning points.

| **Too many turning points** make the work much more difficult!

18.2 Second Preliminary Exercise

Now you know the levers a little bit. In the next exercise we go one step further.

Preparation:

- Delete the first curve that has just been drawn.
- Draw **two lines**, double-click at the intersection:

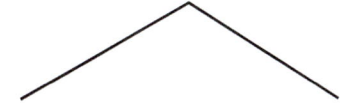

- Convert both lines to **curves**.
  - You can use the shape tool to draw a selection frame to select both lines at once and convert them to curves.

Curves without edges:

Now the point of intersection of the two curves is important, because there, finally, no edge should remain. This is achieved by aligning the levers to a line as shown in the following figure.

- **Bend** the curves as shown to make the levers appear. First touch the curves in the middle and bend them out:

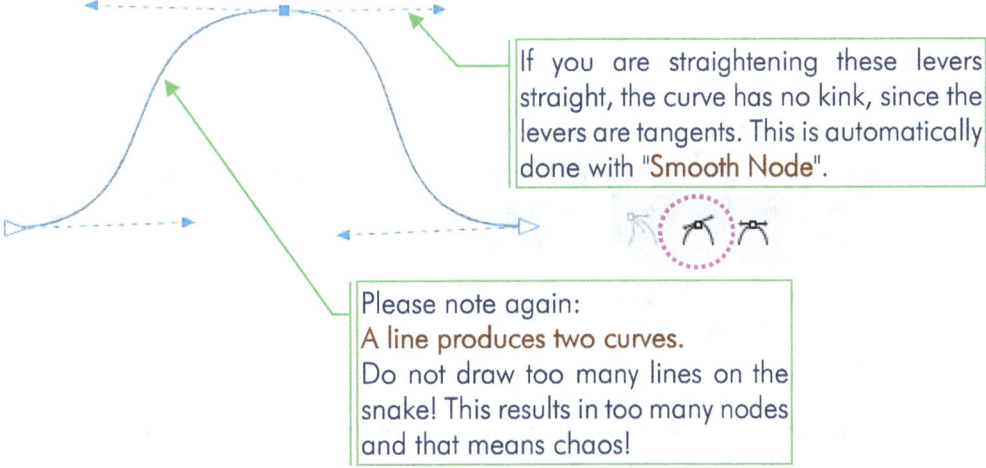

If you are straightening these levers straight, the curve has no kink, since the levers are tangents. This is automatically done with "Smooth Node".

Please note again:
A line produces two curves.
Do not draw too many lines on the snake! This results in too many nodes and that means chaos!

To exercise the levers, we have just **smoothed** a curve by hand. Corel does the same smoothing with the functions mentioned. If these are switched on, you cannot pull an acute angle like the nose.

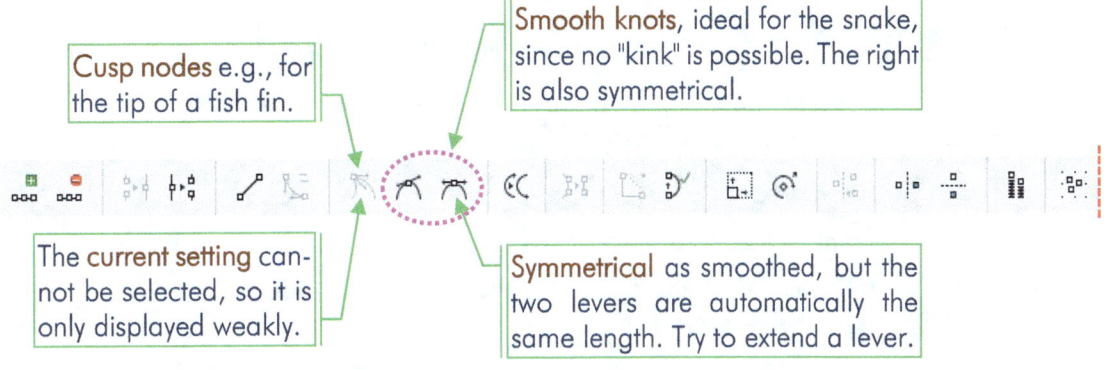

Cusp nodes e.g., for the tip of a fish fin.

Smooth knots, ideal for the snake, since no "kink" is possible. The right is also symmetrical.

The current setting cannot be selected, so it is only displayed weakly.

Symmetrical as smoothed, but the two levers are automatically the same length. Try to extend a lever.

18.3 Serious Case: The Snake

The snake is not a problem if you remember not to draw too many lines. Other points could be supplemented at any time by the + or with a double-click, but too many turning points lead to a chaos of levers.

You will see that the following figure with the red line easily turns into the green snake with round curves.

- Delete the previous curves.
- Draw the red lines by double-clicking on one piece.

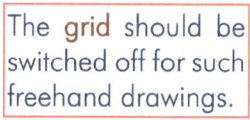

The grid should be switched off for such freehand drawings.

 Either with **lines** =
continue with double-click, stop with single click
or with the **Polyline** = continue with single click and stop with double-click.

- If necessary, move the turning points appropriately.

Convert lines to curves:

- You can **convert** several lines at once to curves by marking them with a large selection frame with the **Shape Tool**, then **switch to curves**.

Select the turning points, and assign the desired type:

- On the head we need pointed points (cusp node), so mark the head with a selection frame and switch to **cusp node** (they are probably already pointed), and the same for the end point.

- Then mark the **fuselage** (without head and end) and select "**smoothed**" in the property bar. The turning points are automatically smoothed, and the desired round contours are created.

> The function "**smoothed**" helps for nice round curves, only at the tip of the tail and at the head are some pointed points necessary.

- **Modify** the curves further until the snake shape fits.
  - ↳ The easiest way to do this is to touch the corners in the middle, not the levers.
- Save as "Snake" – we need this later again for making a flyer.

If it does not go as expected, there are probably still **open points**. Then close these points as described in Chapter 17.5.

What you might need:

- **Add Points**: with double-click (or "+").
- **Delete Points**: Mark the point and click "–" in the Property Bar or on the keyboard.
- **Move Points**: with the **Shape Tool** every time possible.

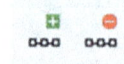

18.4 THE HEAD AND THE POINTS

The head shape is designed just like the snake body:

> By strong zoom convert the lines to curves and buckle out.

The eyes consist of two ellipses:

The easiest way is to draw them first in the empty area next to the head, increasing this area as much as possible.

> Increase line thickness at the outer edge, both fill color. Adjust **colors** for both.
> Finish, then **group** to one eye, rotate and fit in the right place.
> Do not redo the **second eye**, but copy the first (with the right mouse button), then move and then rotate.
> ✏ Or create a horizontally and vertically mirrored copy with **Window/Dockers/Transform** for Scaling and Mirroring.

The hair is the easiest:

> Draw three **lines**, convert them to curves and bend them appropriately.
> Line thickness, color, and round end pieces in the line menu.
> **Group** the three hairs to an object.

The mouth:

> Draw **two lines** one at a time: Click, move mouse away and double-click, and return to the starting point,
> **convert** to curves and bend them appropriately.
> Increase the line **thickness**, select Fill and line color.
> If the filling does not work, close the points.

On the left and right, set **two points**, switch to sharp to make the center part more bulging.

> Finally, supplement the tongue and group all elements.
> Now the mouth can be rotated and positioned correctly.

> **Do not draw on other objects**, but in a vacancy or in a separate drawing. Only when an object is ready, group it and move it to the correct position. Adjust the size and rotation.

We continue in the next chapter with **text and pictures**.

19. TEXT EDITING

Whether it is a poster, a cover page or a promotional brochure, text almost always occurs.

Corel offers two types of text editing:

- The Graphic text with the text tool (which you have done so far) for short texts that can be placed and rotated as desired.
- The Paragraph text to write longer texts as in a text program. Even styles can be assigned.

In the following exercise, we will supplement the text to the snake and will also fit the text to the snake as shown in the picture and in other various ways.

19.1 PRODUCING SHADOWS

- ➢ Write with the Text Tool: AFS.
- ➢ Use the mouse or the property bar to enlarge it, but do not rotate.

A simple monochrome shadow is very nice and is used more often in professional work than special effects.

For this we will copy the text and move it slightly. Then the color is changed for text and shadow and the shadow is finished.

- ➢ For copying and accurate moving, the menu Window/Dockers/Transform with Position is ideal.

With Window/Dockers/Transform exact values can be specified:

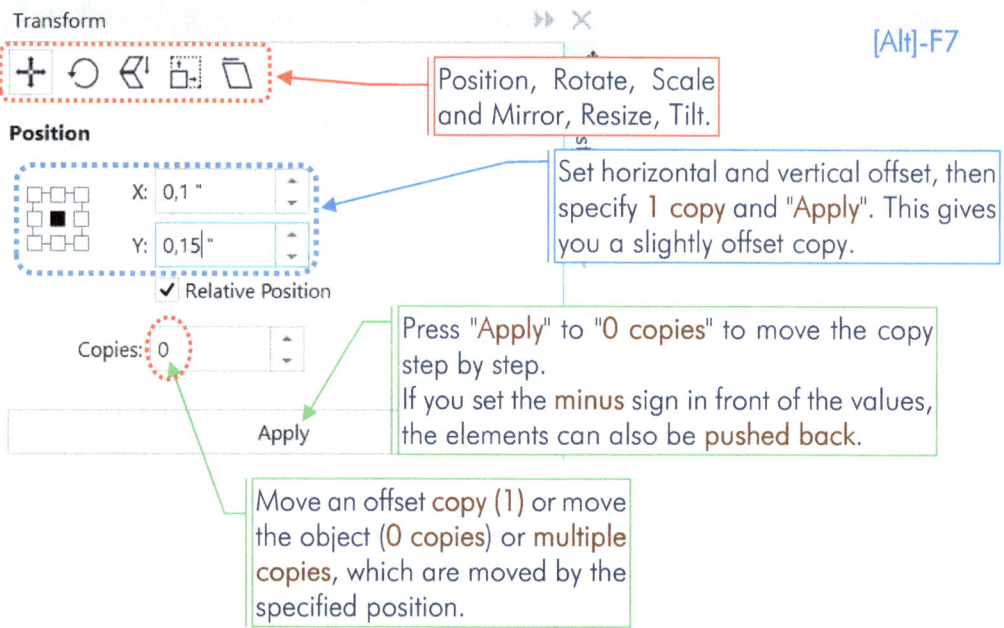

[Alt]-F7

- Move the new object to the back (**Object/Order/Back one**) and change the color.
- The shadow is finished, finally the two different colored texts can be **grouped** into one element.
- Write "**Adventure Fun Sports**" with two empty keys between the words because a special character will be placed there.

We want to turn AFS and Adventure ... at the same angle:

By means of the **Property Bar**, we can rotate different objects at the same angle.

- You can rotate first with the mouse approximately the way you want, and then change it to the next even value in the Property Bar, e.g., to 50 ° instead of 50.317.

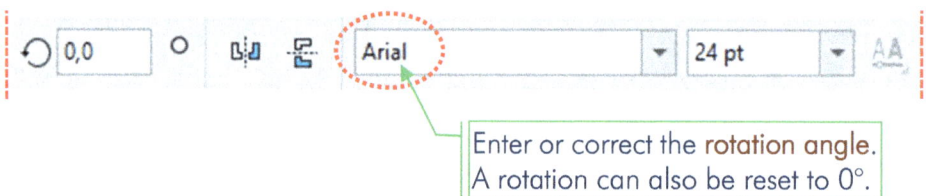

Even with the text selected, the rotation angle is displayed next to the text settings in the property bar.

- Without the Property Bar, the option remains over this handy menu **Window/Dockers/Transform** by Rotate.
  - Here, for example, set a rotation of 10 °, then press "**Assign**" several times until the angle of rotation fits.
  - The angle of rotation is thus known and can be assigned exactly the same to other objects.

19.2 Insert Special Characters

Now we insert symbol fonts between: Adventure Fun Sports

- ➤ Choose the Text Tool and set the cursor between two words (we have prepared with two space bars between the words).
- ➤ With Text/Glyphen or [Ctrl]-[F11] you can open the special character window,
- ➤ there you can select a special font, e.g., Wingdings. You can drag a symbol on the text or insert with double-click.
  - ★ Move the cursor to the next position with the directional buttons and double-click on the symbol again.

Adventure ➲ Fun➲ Sports

19.3 Color Variety

In this text, the initial letters are to be displayed in a different color:

- ➤ Select Text Tool, click on text and mark the first letter of adventure, then use the mouse to assign a different color from the color palette.

Marking a letter, you have these possibilities:

- ♦ With the mouse, it requires fingertip feeling to mark exactly one letter.
- ♦ Holding down the [Shift] key and a directional key will make it easier.
  - ✎ And you can also unmark if you have marked too much as long as you hold down the [Shift] key with the directional key in other direction.

The color is only changed for the selected text.

19.4 Align Text to an Object

With this function "Fit Text to Path", text can be written to an object, e.g., at our snake. Let's try it:

- ➤ The grouping of the snake must be cancelled beforehand.
- ➤ Click on the text "Adventure ..." and select Text/Fit Text to Path.
- ➤ The mouse arrow changes to a bigger arrow, when you move the mouse near the snake, a preview is displayed.

- ✎ Move the mouse near the queue until arranged as desired, then confirm with a mouse click.
- ✎ The initial position and the distance from the route can be subsequently adjusted in the Property Bar.

You can change the arrangement at any time in the Property Bar if text and object are selected:

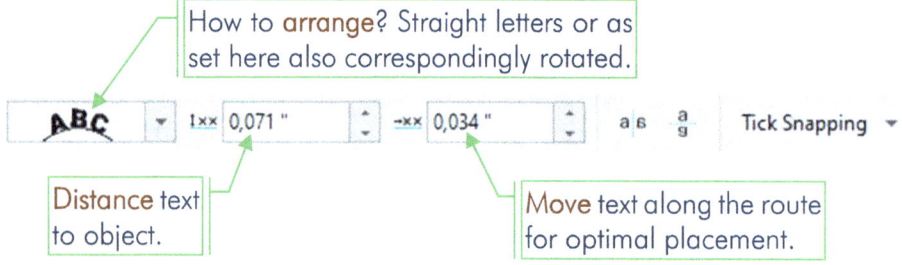

Tick Snapping:

- For example, if set at 5mm, the target position can still be freely selected with the mouse, but at a distance of 5mm, this locks a little, even afterwards during the movement.

If the text is placed on the wrong side, mirror it:
Text can also be arranged below.

19.5 Add The Address

Fill in the address at the bottom of the picture.

➢ Write the Headline separate and fit left and right side to the Guidelines.

➢ Then make two blocks of Paragraph Text, align one to the left Guideline and text left aligned, the other to the right Guideline and the text inside right-aligned.

✎ The feature with Paragraph Text is so you can align easy and exactly to left and right Guideline. With Graphic Text this is not easy to adjust exactly because Corel counts coordinates for the center point of it.

Adventure ➲ Fun ➲ Sports Ltd.

125 Barclay Street
New York, NY 10007
United States

Phone: (212) 888-1111
Fax: (212) 888-1114
www.adv-fun-sports.com
Email: sample@adv-fun-sports.com

19.6 Other Adjustments for Text

The Property Bar is very handy, but only the most important settings are available. The Property Bar for text you'll find in Chapter 11.1.1.

- The complete menu with all settings for text can be found on these paths:
  - ✎ right mouse button on the text, then Properties
  - ✎ or open with Window/Toolbar/Text the toolbar for text
  - ✎ or Text/Text: in this menu you will also find the position or fractional numbers, the shortcut [Ctrl]-T opens this menu, too,
  - ✎ or the icon shown on the left, to be found on the far right in the property bar.

[Ctrl]-t

This extensive and unfortunately confusing setting menu for text will be presented on the next page.

The Docker Text/Text:

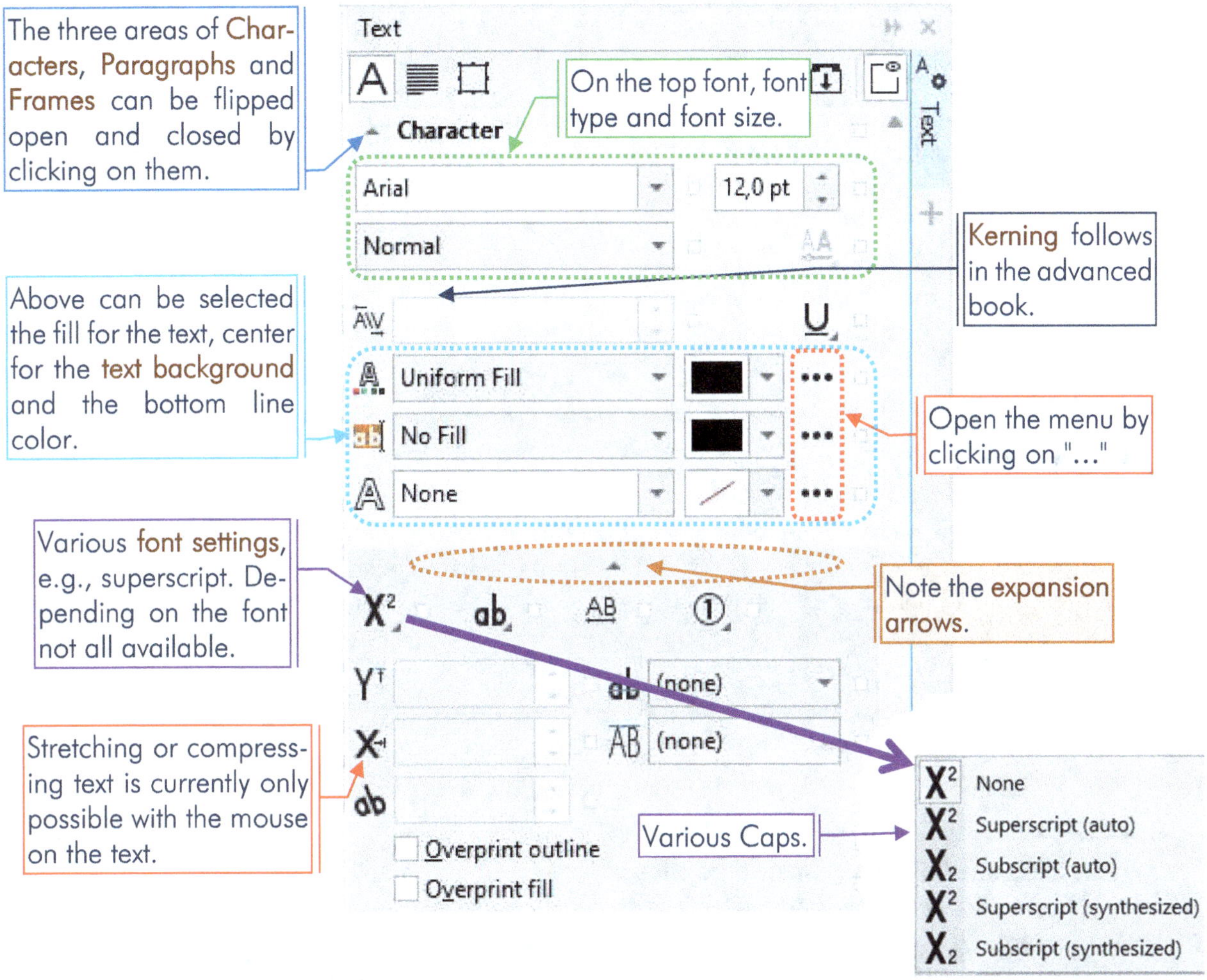

The three areas of Characters, Paragraphs and Frames can be flipped open and closed by clicking on them.
Text
Character
On the top font, font type and font size.
Arial
12,0 pt
Normal
Kerning follows in the advanced book.
Above can be selected the fill for the text, center for the text background and the bottom line color.
Uniform Fill
No Fill
None
Open the menu by clicking on "..."
Various font settings, e.g., superscript. Depending on the font not all available.
Note the expansion arrows.
(none)
(none)
Stretching or compressing text is currently only possible with the mouse on the text.
Overprint outline
Overprint fill
Various Caps.
None
Superscript (auto)
Subscript (auto)
Superscript (synthesized)
Subscript (synthesized)

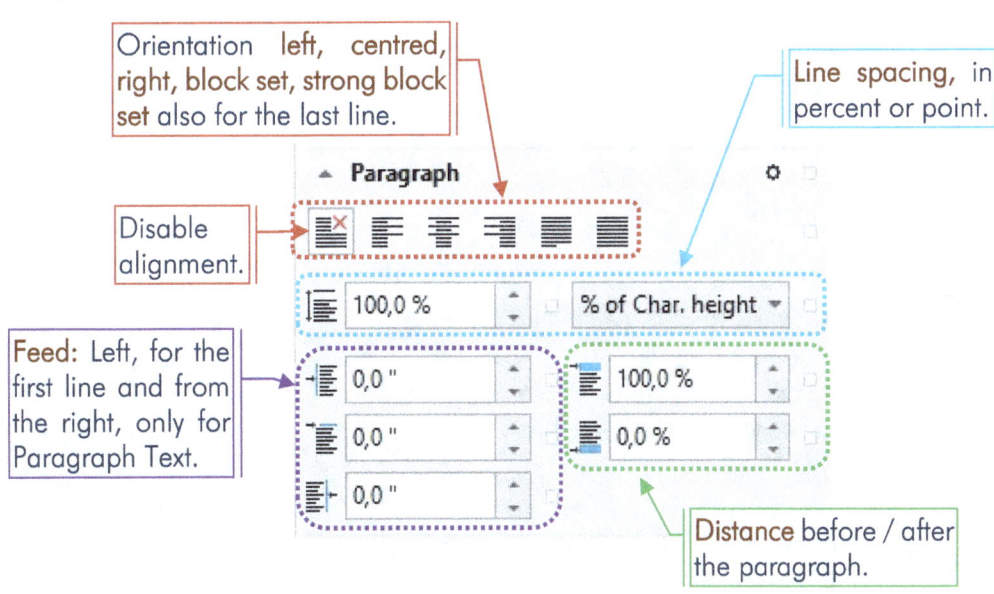

Paragraph formatting further down in the menu, a lot only works with paragraph text:

Orientation left, centred, right, block set, strong block set also for the last line.
Line spacing, in percent or point.
Paragraph
Disable alignment.
100,0 %
% of Char. height
Feed: Left, for the first line and from the right, only for Paragraph Text.
0,0 "
0,0 "
0,0 "
100,0 %
0,0 %
Distance before / after the paragraph.

The above menu is also accessible via Windows/Dockers/Text or with [Ctrl] -T.

More about the text settings:

- The setting in **percentage of the character size** has the advantage that the setting is adapted automatically if you change the font size.

- Depending on the font selected, not all options are possible, e.g., some fonts cannot be set bold or italic.

- Text/Text Properties, [Ctrl]-[Shift]-T or, if text is marked, in the Property Bar ab|:

    ↳ This opens a small text screen (**text editor**) in which you can correct, write and format the text - helpful if the text is distorted with effects.

Ctrl-Shift-T

ab|

19.7 OTHER TEXT HELPS

- Corel provides all the tools of a good word processing program that you will find in **Text/Writing Tools (not available by Essentials)**:

    ↳ a **Spell Checker**,

    ↳ a **Grammar Checker** and

    ↳ **Thesaurus**, a dictionary for synonyms. Here you can search for similar terms to a word.

    ↳ the **QuickCorrect**, which opens a window in which this automatic correction can be adjusted,

    ↳ the **language** can also be chosen here so that the spelling check also works for foreign-language texts.

About QuickCorrect:

The **QuickCorrect** is similar the **AutoCorrect** in MS Word.

- With "**Capitalize first letter of sentences**" the first letter of a sentence is also capitalized after each abbreviation, since CorelDRAW starts a new sentence after each point. This option is disabled for Corel by default. If the capitalization is corrected once after an abbreviation, Corel accepts this.

- With "**Change straight quotes to typographic quotes**" Corel changes to "abc" instead of "abc".

- "**Replace text while typing**" automatically replaces the standard errors in the list below with the entered texts.

    ↳ Other abbreviations, e.g., for a company name, can be supplemented. In the case of "**Replace:**", enter an abbreviation or an incorrect spelling, enter the detailed or correct spelling in "**With:**" and save it with "**Add**".

    ↳ If you often have unwanted replacements, you should **disable** this feature. If you want to use this function, it is worthwhile to maintain the replacement list.

20. THE PARAGRAPH TEXT

Paragraph text is the second type of text editing in CorelDRAW. While **graphic text** behaves as a drawing element, **paragraph text** is arranged in a text frame.

Paragraph text is, so to speak, a small text program, which we can open in a Corel graphic. This text is set within a frame for the delineation.

paragraph text for big amounts of text.

You start the Paragraph Text as follows:

- Press as usual the text symbol. Then:
    - Click in the drawing to write **Graphic Text** or
    - draw a Paragraph Text frame like a rectangle with the mouse button pressed.
- **Caution**, draw a Paragraph frame only if this is the intention.
    - Otherwise, immediately switch back from the **Text Tool** to the **Pick Tool** arrow, otherwise you would use the text tool instead of the Pick Tool and create an empty text frame.

Empty paragraph text frames are indicated by dashed lines. Delete any accidentally drawn frames: **Click on it with Pick Tool – [Del]**.

Empty Paragraph Text frames: Paragraph Text frames with text:

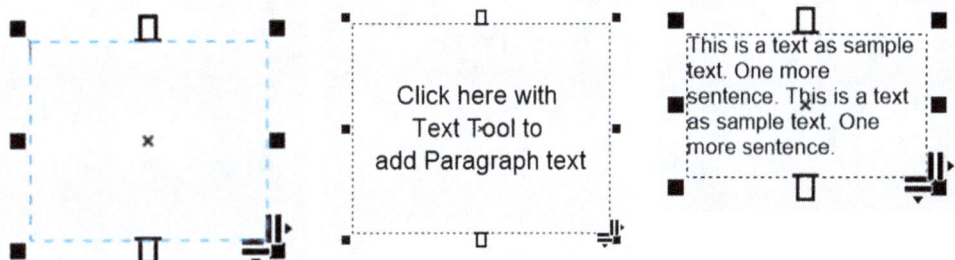

20.1 CONVERTING TEXT

You can convert graphic text to paragraph text and vice versa. This is displayed in the Text Menu, in the scrolling menu with the right mouse button pressed over text or with the keyboard truncation [Ctrl]-F8.

[Ctrl]-F8

Conditions:

- Mark the text with the **Pick Tool**, not with the Text Tool.
- With **Paragraph text**, the text frame does not have to be so big that the text is completely visible.

20.2 Exercise: Business Card

To get a better understanding of the Paragraph Text, we will create a small business card. This is how it will go:

- New drawing, size 80x60 mm or 30"x20", adjust the grid to 1 mm or 0.2" distance – for a small drawing we need a fine grid distance.

Because we are printing on colored paper, we choose a paper color:

- Layout/Page Background, then choose with "Solid" the color palette Pantone CMYK Coated by Process.

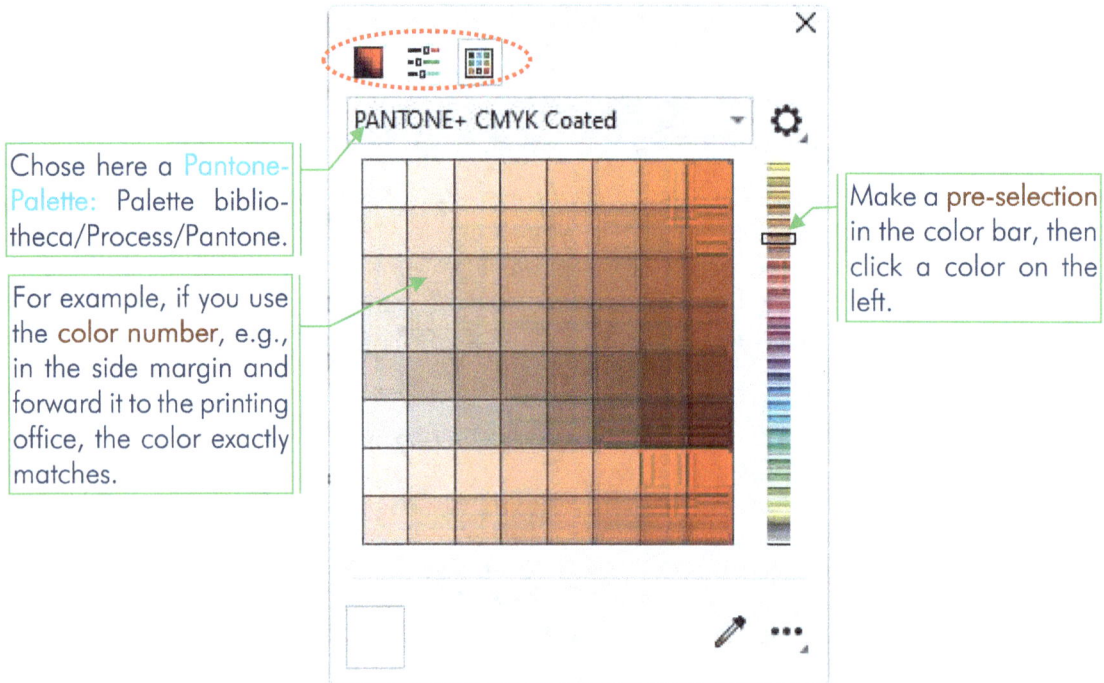

Chose here a Pantone-Palette: Palette bibliotheca/Process/Pantone.

For example, if you use the color number, e.g., in the side margin and forward it to the printing office, the color exactly matches.

Make a pre-selection in the color bar, then click a color on the left.

- Switch off "Print and export background", so that the set paper color is not printed – if the print shop will use paper in this color.
  - It is a good practice to better assess ink composition on the screen when printing on colored paper.

The two lines above and below are simple rectangles with a color gradient fill:

- Place the Guidelines 4 mm or 1.5" apart from the side edge.
- Draw a rectangle, turn the outline off (with the right mouse button at the top of the color palette with the X) and
- fill with a gradient color filling similar to the one shown.

Now we will copy and flip the rectangle once, which gives the copy a precisely swapped color fill (Object/Transform/Scale and Mirror).

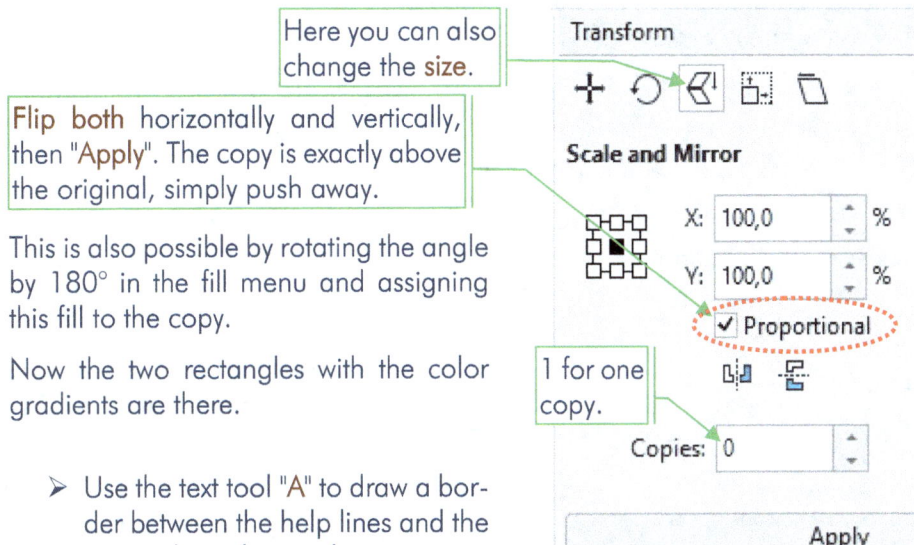

Here you can also change the size.

Flip both horizontally and vertically, then "Apply". The copy is exactly above the original, simply push away.

This is also possible by rotating the angle by 180° in the fill menu and assigning this fill to the copy.

Now the two rectangles with the color gradients are there.

1 for one copy.

> Use the text tool "A" to draw a border between the help lines and the rectangle and enter the text.

↳ Since this frame is docked to the left and right of the help lines, the centering of the text is easier than with the graphic text.

20.3 Handling with the Paragraph Text Frames

- ◆ Too much or too big of text or a too small text frame will cause the text to be displayed only partially or not.
  - ↳ Always pull the frame down and right much larger than necessary until the text is set correctly. Only if the text is finished, then reduce the size of the text frame.
  - ↳ An alternative is the command "Text/Paragraph Text Frame/Fit Text to Frame", also accessible by right-clicking on the frame, so the font size is automatically adjusted so that the text fills the frame.

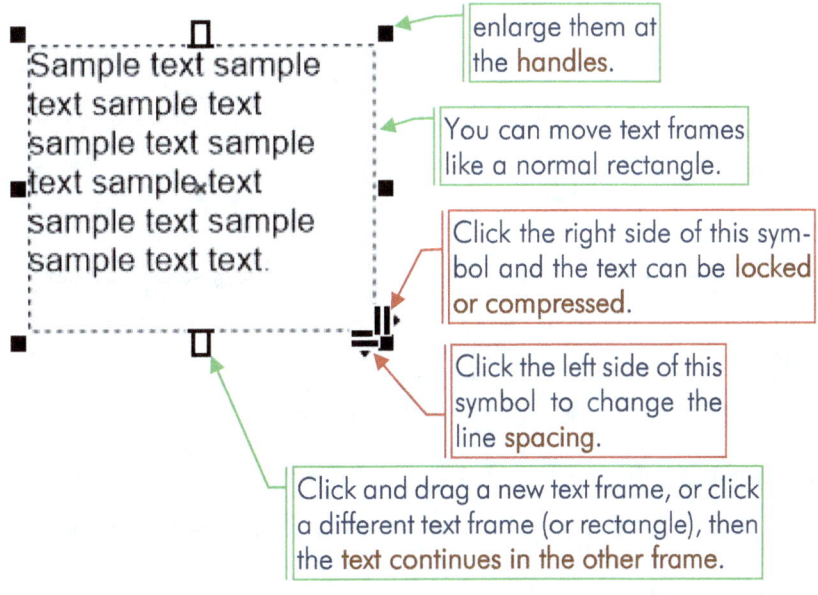

enlarge them at the handles.

You can move text frames like a normal rectangle.

Click the right side of this symbol and the text can be locked or compressed.

Click the left side of this symbol to change the line spacing.

Click and drag a new text frame, or click a different text frame (or rectangle), then the text continues in the other frame.

> Format the business card as shown. Always select the appropriate text.

20.4 Print from CorelDraw

As in any program, you can print on these paths:
File/Print with the Symbol / [Ctrl]-P.

- On the tab "General", the printer can be selected and the desired print quality can be set by "Preferences…".
- With "Page:" you can choose Landscape or Portrait.

With the "Home & Student" and Essentials Edition, you have an easier print menu; there you can only choose with "Imposition layout" some preferences for label print. By the full edition you can set the quantity of rows and columns with "Page Layout".

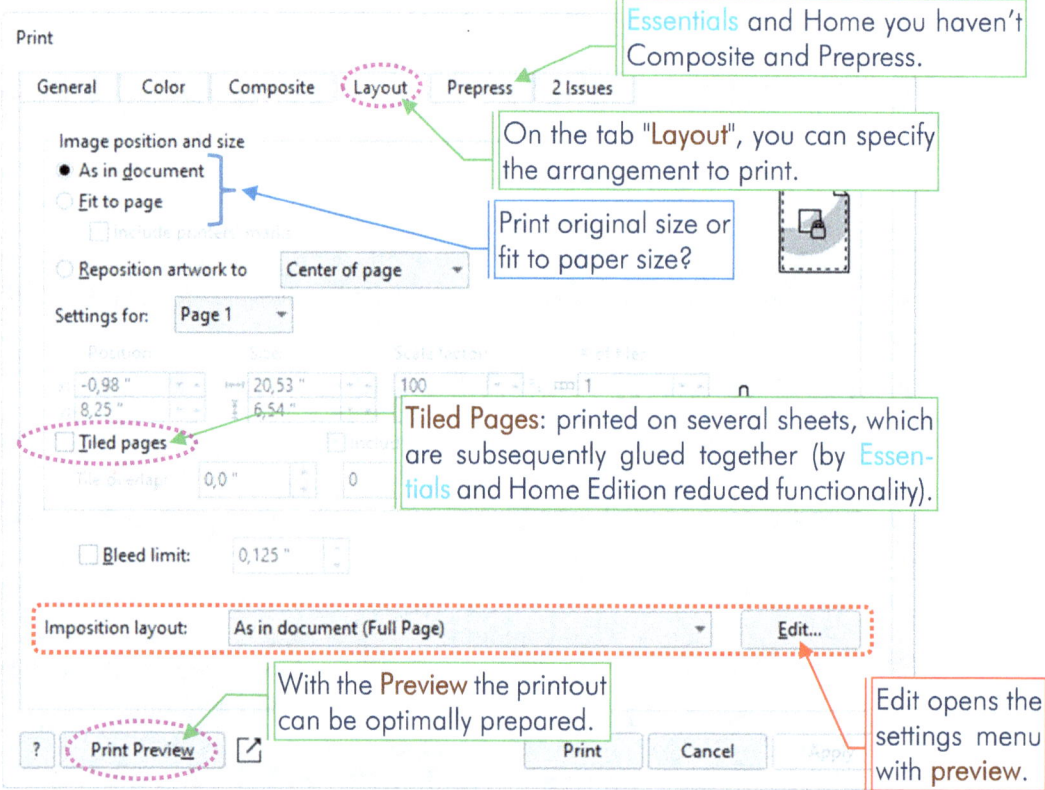

Choose "Edit" by Imposition Layout for the settings (not by Essentials, Home):

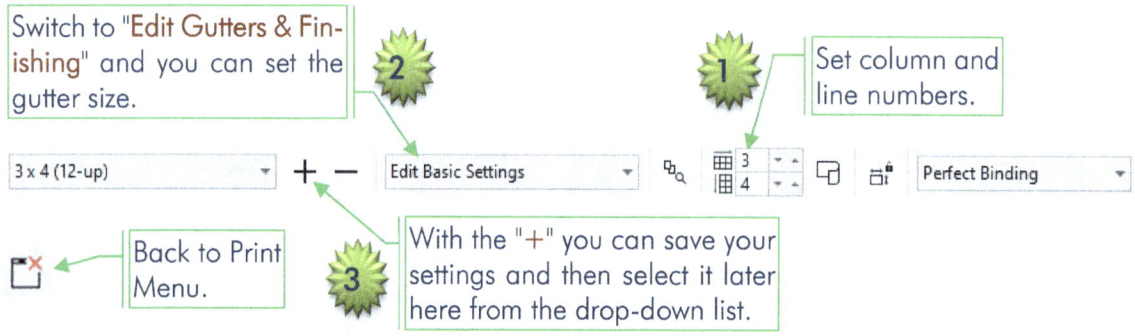

➢ Close this menu, switch on the Preview and it if all matches, print it out.

Another method, with a bit of manual work, but more obvious, is to specify the columns and lines with Guidelines, and to copy the first completed business card into the other cells before printing, would also go automatically with the transform menu.

Chapter 21

21. PICTURES AND TEXT

You already know the word processing, including Paragraph text, the snake is already drawn and how pictures are inserted has already been explained in the exercise on page 89. Consequently, the prospectus should now be finished without any problems.

It is supposed to be a folded sheet with 5 folded columns. So that the exercise does not take too long, this is cut here on three sides. And the original images were replaced by images from the Web.

➢ Open the exercise Snake from Chapter 18 and save it under the name AFS folder.

➢ Instead of one page, we now need to set up three, that is, page format three times as wide as 300 mm.

➢ You can now set the following vertical Guidelines: 10, 90/110, 190/210, 290. In the case of known coordinates, the Guideline menu is advantageous: Right mouse button on the ruler, then select "Guidelines Setup…".

➢ Mark the snake side (snake and address text) with a large marking frame (Pick Tool) and drag it to the right page.

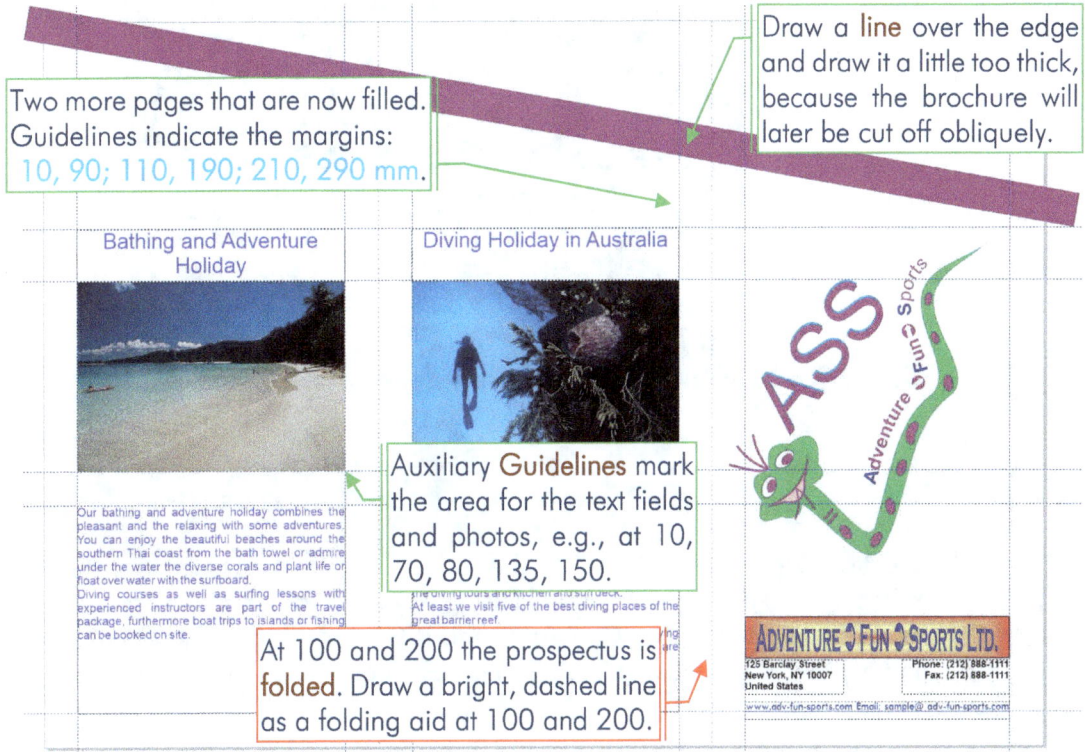

21.1 Insert Photos

Now we have three sides, two of which are still empty.

> Now we search for photos on the Internet: start an **Internet browser** and search e.g., by www.msn.com or www.google.com, matching photos for our flyer as "**travel**" or "**beach**" or "**scuba**" and switch to "**photos**".

> Open suitable photos, copy with **right mouse button/copy** and insert in Corel, also with right mouse button, [Ctrl]-v or this icon:

> If you save the photos on your hard drive, you could insert it in CorelDRAW the following ways: using the symbol "**Import**", from **Corel Assets**, or open the folder in the **Windows Explorer** and drag into CorelDRAW.

> Adjust the size roughly and move it to the desired position with the left top handle matching to the Guidelines, then finish by moving the size to the right bottom Guideline corner.

> Change the **size of images** only at the corner points, otherwise the size ratio will be distorted. If this happens, immediately undo or re-import the image.

Arrangement of sample pictures:

Notice: Do not look for the original example photos, but similar ones from the Internet.

Move first to this corner point of the Guidelines.

Second to this corner point of the Guidelines.

Attention! Only change the size at the **corner point**; if you use the central handles at the top/bottom and left/right, you will distort the image, i.e., change the width to height ratio. This is OK for some images, but another method of making images fit is described in the next chapter.

21.2 Cut Edge Areas of Photos

Most of the time the size does not fit into our image area and photos should not simply be widened or compressed as this would distort the aspect ratio.

Then we cut the edge areas with the Shape or Crop Tool:

Use the Shape Tool to drag the edge point to the help line corner to cut the image.

Also possible with the Crop Tool to mark the remaining area and confirm with return.

21.3 Insert Paragraph Text

➢ Drag a Guideline over the first image so that all the sets of text frames can be arranged at the same height, then set them.

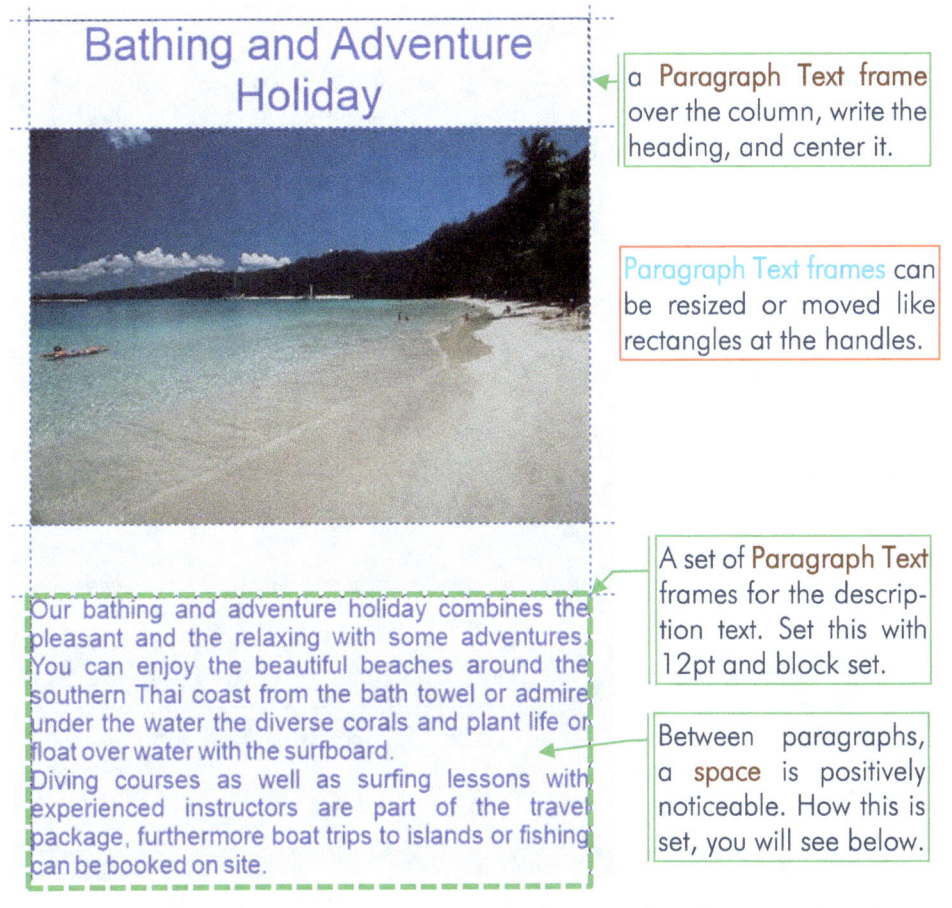

a Paragraph Text frame over the column, write the heading, and center it.

Paragraph Text frames can be resized or moved like rectangles at the handles.

A set of Paragraph Text frames for the description text. Set this with 12pt and block set.

Between paragraphs, a space is positively noticeable. How this is set, you will see below.

21.4 Text Formatting and Hyphenation

You can format the Paragraph Text similar to the Graphic Text, except that all setting options for a good writing program are available for the Paragraph Text. You will find most of the settings in the Properties bar.

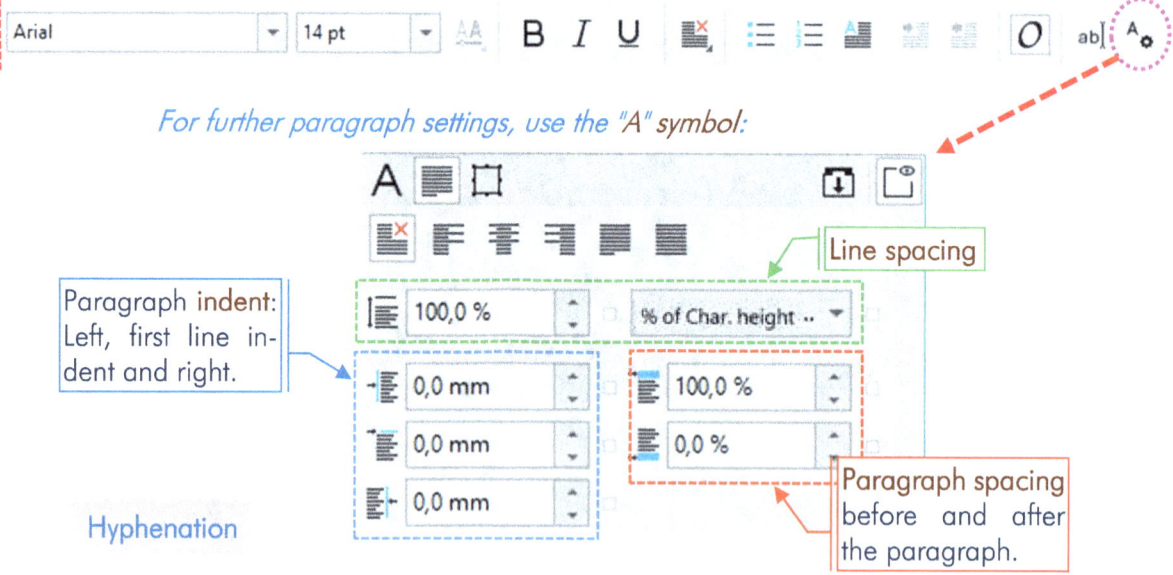

For further paragraph settings, use the "A" symbol:

- Line spacing
- Paragraph indent: Left, first line indent and right.
- Paragraph spacing before and after the paragraph.
- Hyphenation

By Text/Use Hyphenation (not available by Essentials / Home) you can activate it, which is particularly recommended for Paragraph Text.

21.5 Add a Page

The back of the page will be filled with text and images like the first page, where we insert a normal page and print it later in two stages: first the front, turn the paper, and then the backside unless the printer can duplex.

At the bottom left you can add (empty) pages:

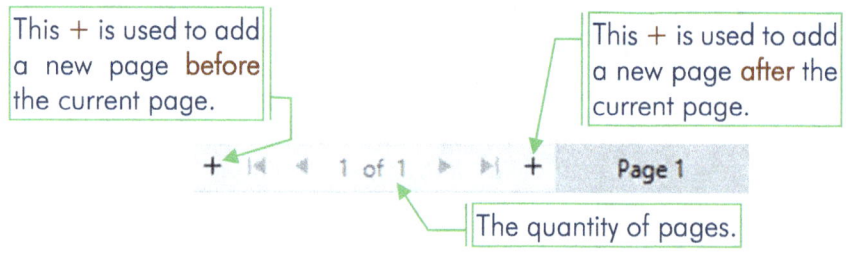

- This + is used to add a new page before the current page.
- This + is used to add a new page after the current page.
- The quantity of pages.

➤ Add another page. If done, you can change the pages at the bottom of the page:

- To the last page.
- Click to select a page.

➤ Copy the top line to the back and mirror it.

➤ Add more photos from the Internet and set in the desired positions, then add sample text as shown, matching your pictures, of course.

Find matching photos and arrange them in the columns:

The Dream of Flying	Get out into Nature

Get into the air! Whether with the paraglider, parachute, or as a glider, a paragliding safari, with hot air balloon, bungee jumping or body flying.	Riding with the horse or with the engine sled in Canada, Germany, Austria, Italy, France, USA etc. Climbing, adventure camps, spelunking (caves) etc.

Set the font size, type etc. again and again manually? First copy a selected text frame, then overwrite the text, or copy the text settings with Edit/Copy Properties From...

As in a good writing program, we can store the text settings in one style and assign them to other paragraphs as often as you want. This is presented in our progress book filled with more professional exercises.

21.6 Edit Photos

In CorelDRAW, you can cut the edges of the image with the Shape Tool, while marking two handles with a selection frame so that it is not crooked.

Photo-Paint

With Effects/Adjust you'll find the commands to change the brightness, contrast and more and with Bitmaps you'll find all effects for photos from Corel Photo-Paint. In our book about Corel PHOTO-PAINT you will find a description of these numerous effects for photos. If you press the right mouse button on a picture and select Edit bitmap, PHOTO-PAINT is started.

The important icons of the Property bar for photos in CorelDRAW:

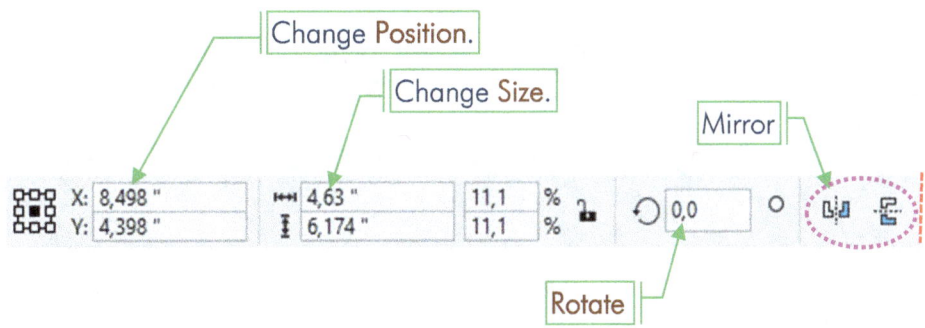

Other symbols on the right side:

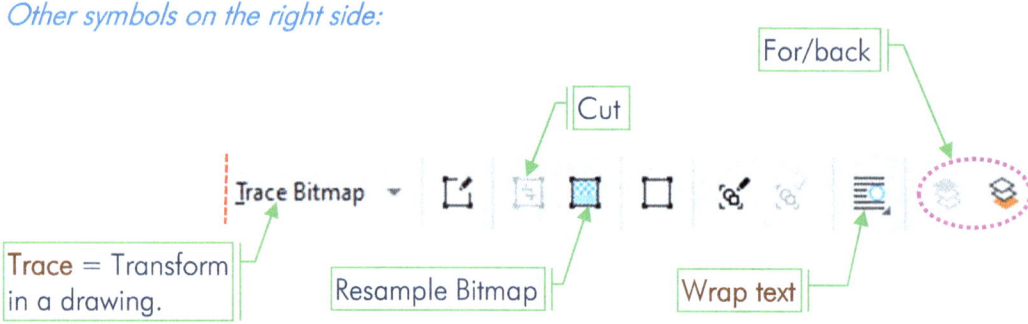

- **Rotate:** images can be rotated, which is also possible with the mouse as with any other element.

- **Photo-Paint** is the program for photos. All images (photos) in the computer are so-called pixel images. Therefore, editing is quite different from CorelDRAW, so a separate program is used. More about Corel PHOTO-PAINT in our book on this program.

- **Vectorize:** This allows pixel images to be converted into vector drawings, which means that photos can be converted into graphics, which usually does not yield any results that would be suitable for further processing since too many lines and turning points are created.

In the menu Bitmaps:

- **Resample:** a menu appears in which you can reduce the size or resolution (= number of pixels = dpi = dots per inch) of a photo, which naturally also decreases the quality (sharpness) in addition to the file size.

- **Bitmap Mask** (not by **Essentials**): in the window that appears, you can use the Eyedropper Tool to pick up colors from the image to hide these colors.
    - ✏ This is convenient to hide e.g., a largely monochrome background.   **Transparent**
    - ✏ The reverse way that the recorded colors remain visible is also possible.

- Right mouse click/**Wrap Paragraph Text**: You can select whether the text is to run outside or over (= every click changes) for graphic elements or photos. Over the photo e.g., to use an image as a background.

Fifth Part

for Text and Extrusion

22. EFFECTS FOR TEXT

For a better overview, we begin with the effects, which are mainly suitable for text. Further effects follow in the progress band.

> **Copy** each sample text a few times so you have enough material to try out!

22.1 INTERACTIVE EFFECTS

Most of the effects can be found as interactive menus on the left in the toolbox:

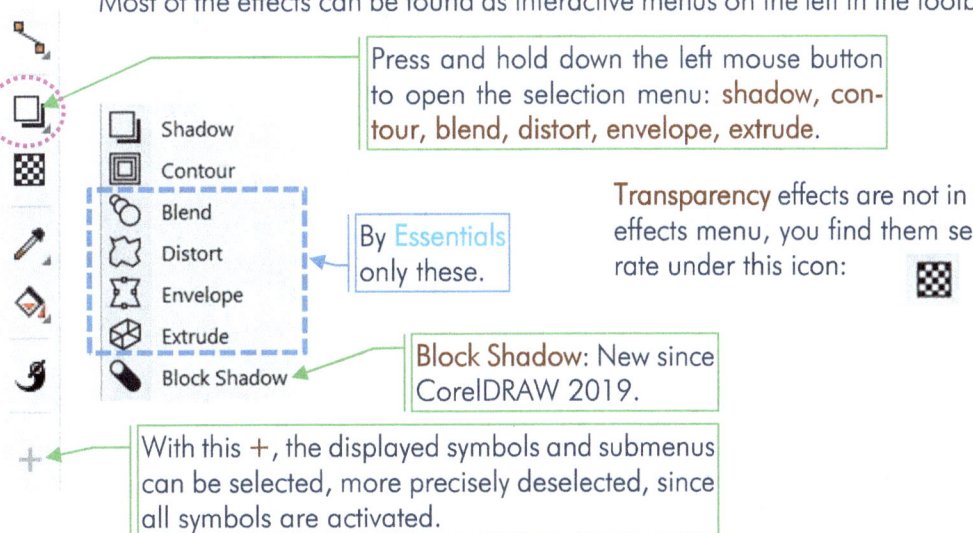

In these interactive menus, you can specify the settings in the property bar or by holding down the left mouse button.

The old method by means of a command for effects is however at the beginning at least more clearly, since a menu is opened, in which the setting possibilities are clearly recognizable.

Therefore, we start with the **Effects menu**, the interactive commands are described in the progress band, but can also be applied without guidance if the effects are known.

Examples of the interactive effects and their applications can be found in Chapter 16 on page 95.

22.2 Move Letters

The easiest effect: letters can be positioned anywhere with the left mouse button (only in graphic text).

> ➢ New graphic and write as Graphic Text: Hello! Copy it a couple times.
>
> ➢ Choose the Shape Tool and you can move letters at the handle points.

Use the Shape Tool to pull letters apart:

For multi-line text, you can change the line spacing here.

At this symbol, text can be stretched or compressed.

22.3 Add Perspective

> ➢ Choose another copy of the sample text.
>
> ➢ Start with: Object/Perspective/Add Perspective:

Corel switches to the shape tool and you can move points with the mouse the corner so that a perspective can be set.

Notice the vanishing point, which can also be moved with the mouse.
The two lines of perspective converge into this vanishing point.

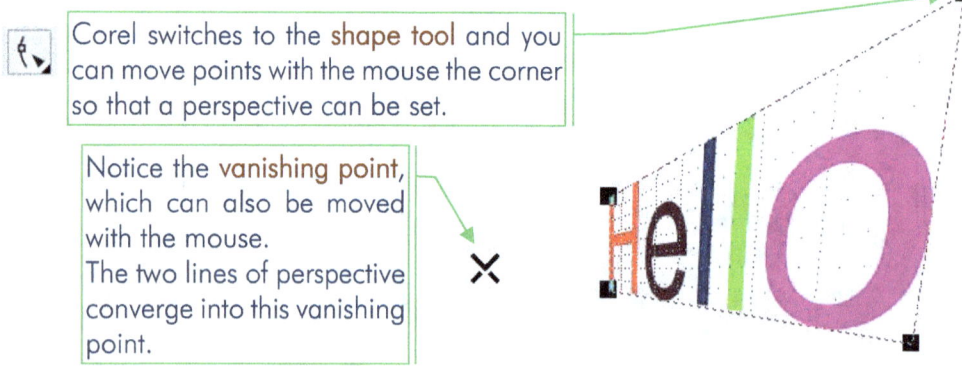

With Object/Perspective/Add Perspective you can remove them at any time.

22.4 THE ENVELOPE EFFECT

- Write "Trumpet" and start with **Effects/Envelope** from the tool bar left side.

- Now you can modify the envelope at the handles.

  - NOTE: If you want a straight envelope, you can delete the turning points in the middle.

Further settings you find in the Property Bar:

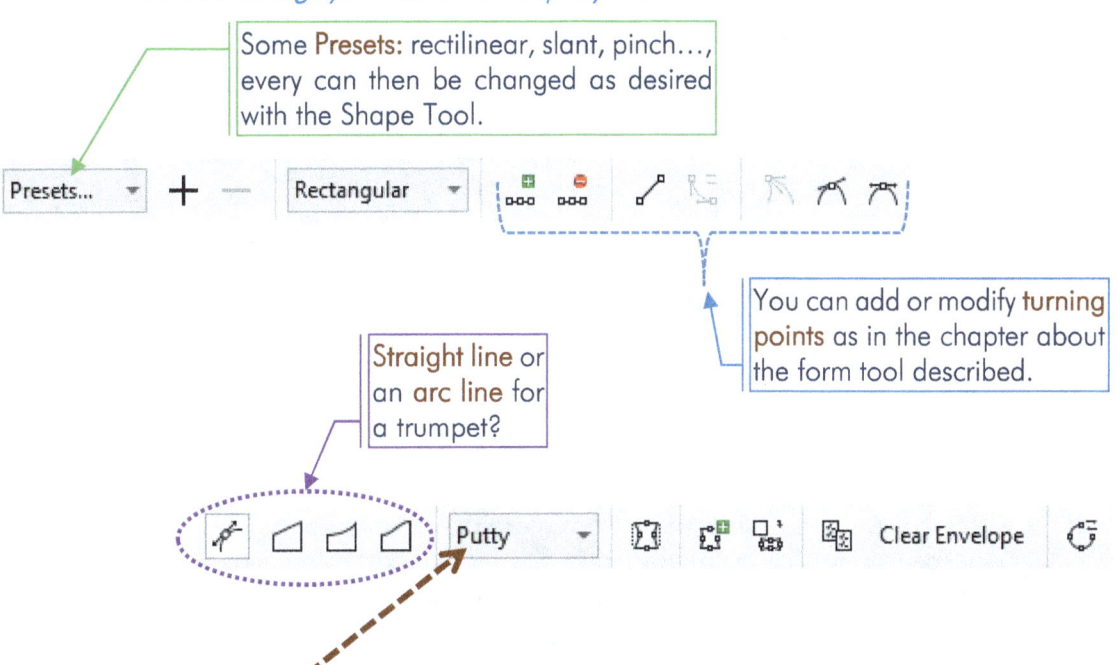

Some **Presets**: rectilinear, slant, pinch…, every can then be changed as desired with the Shape Tool.

You can add or modify **turning points** as in the chapter about the form tool described.

Straight line or an arc line for a trumpet?

Instead, Putty (elastic) you have you have these possibilities: horizontal, vertical, original:

Horizontal: the text is adapted to the envelope horizontally. Mostly illegible result.	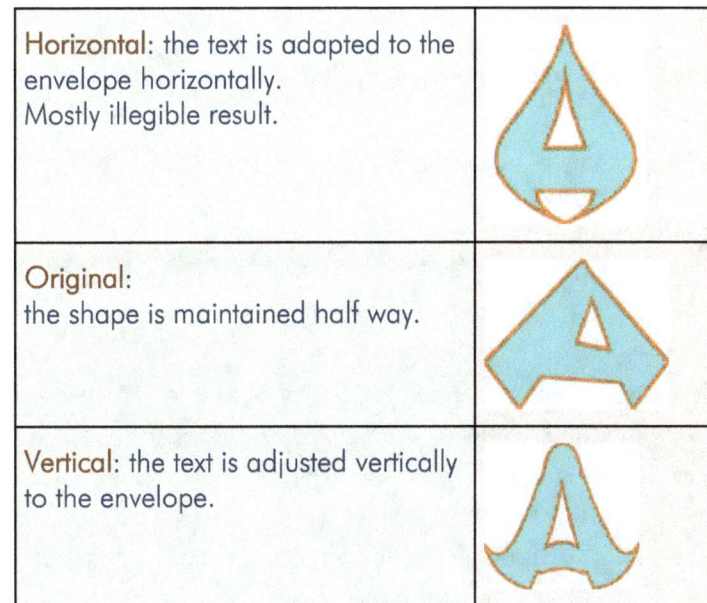
Original: the shape is maintained half way.	
Vertical: the text is adjusted vertically to the envelope.	

22.5 Contour (not by Essentials)

Here we can create different colored steps around the object or within it. Contour is available twice in the Effects menu, with the upper vectorization contours, in this case the lower one, or [Ctrl]-[F9] or from the Effects Icon in the Toolbar left side.

➢ Select a new example text, then Effects/Contour (in the menu the lower contour):

To centre, inside or outside.

Steps = Number of contours (stripes).
Offset = Width of strips.

Unfortunately, Corel always switches back to "in", so that an error message "steps too small" appears, just confirm and click again "out".

Contour outside with red text color:

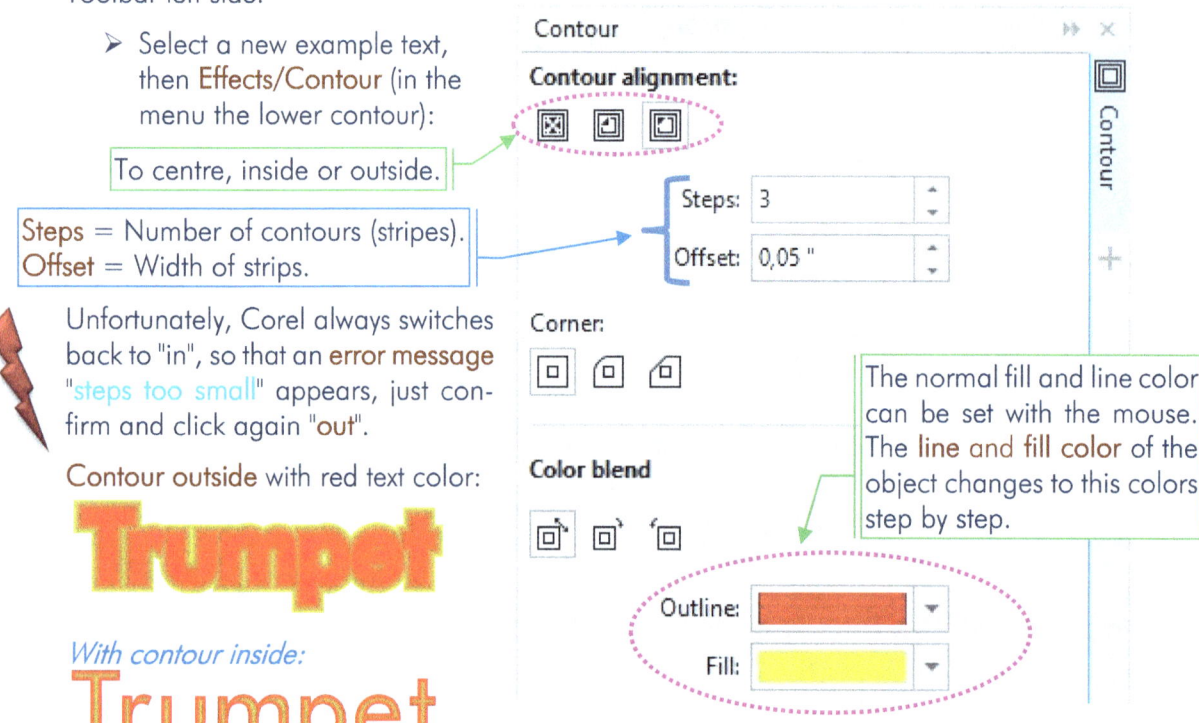

The normal fill and line color can be set with the mouse. The line and fill color of the object changes to this colors step by step.

With contour inside:

Trumpet

- ♦ **To Center**: Corel automatically creates as many contours (steps) as needed to match with the specified width (Contour offset). Therefore, the number of steps cannot be selected but only the width.

- ♦ Many steps with a small distance lead to soft color traces.

- ➢ Start with a contour outward to see the effect.

The Colors:

Here you can choose the way through the color disk from object color to Contour fill color:

The colors of the stripes change from the filling color of the object to the fill color choose in above contour menu, same for the line color.

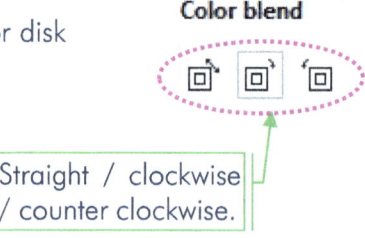

Straight / clockwise / counter clockwise.

Possible Problems:

- ♦ Contours inwards do not seem to go if the distance is set too high! Even to think of a line makes the filling color unrecognizable.
  - ↪ Possibly start with a contour outward, in order to be able to recognize the width of the strips, then try inward.
  - ↪ Increase as much as possible to see the effect, especially with a contour inward.

23. Extrusion

Finally! The classic effect. We will go through all of the settings.

➢ Write the sample text **EX** and set a very large font for it.

➢ **Copy** this text several times to have some exercise material.

> The **Effects/Extrude menu** can only be used after an extrusion has been assigned to an object with the extrude symbol while holding down the mouse button.

23.1 The Depth of the Extrusion

The setting options are divided into some menus. First the depth.

➢ Switch to extrusion on the left side of the effects, then specify the extrusion with the mouse button pressed down from the EX-object:

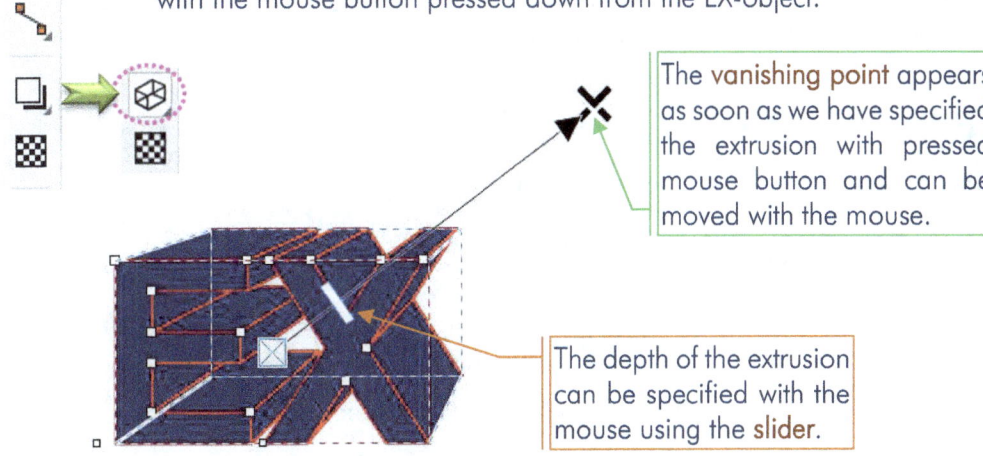

The vanishing point appears as soon as we have specified the extrusion with pressed mouse button and can be moved with the mouse.

The depth of the extrusion can be specified with the mouse using the slider.

The settings in the property bar:

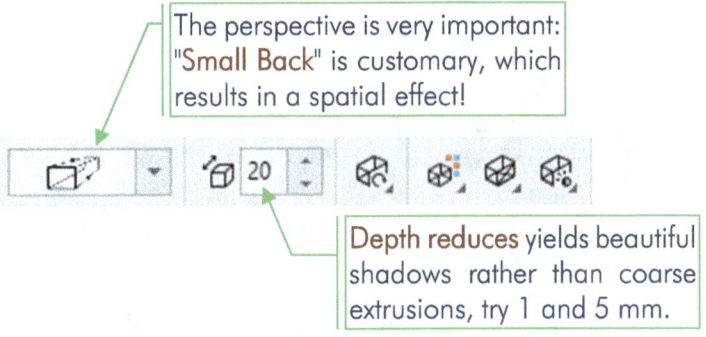

The perspective is very important: "Small Back" is customary, which results in a spatial effect!

Depth reduces yields beautiful shadows rather than coarse extrusions, try 1 and 5 mm.

With color the extrusion is particularly beautiful - follow immediately.

23.2 THE COLOR

Extrusions are only really beautiful with colors.

➢ Choose the fill color from the color palette with the left mouse click, the line color with the right. In addition, the color for the extruded surface can be set in the property bar on this icon:

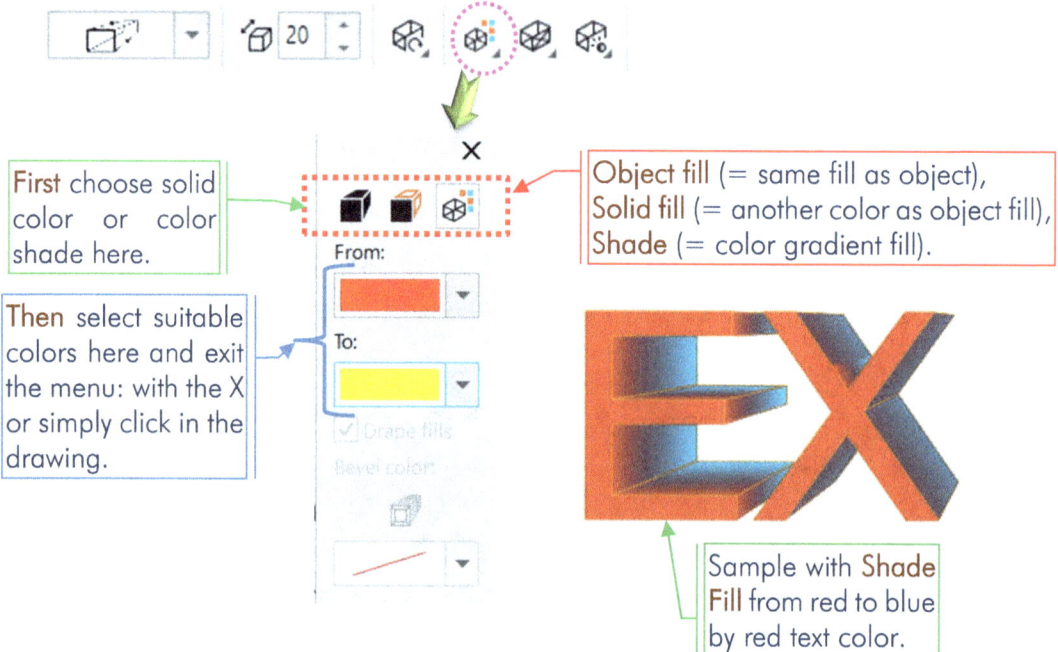

First choose solid color or color shade here.

Then select suitable colors here and exit the menu: with the X or simply click in the drawing.

Object fill (= same fill as object),
Solid fill (= another color as object fill),
Shade (= color gradient fill).

Sample with Shade Fill from red to blue by red text color.

➢ Try a gradient and set two different colors, additionally choose the appropriate object color and line color.

23.3 THE ROTATION

Objects can be rotated on the second card:

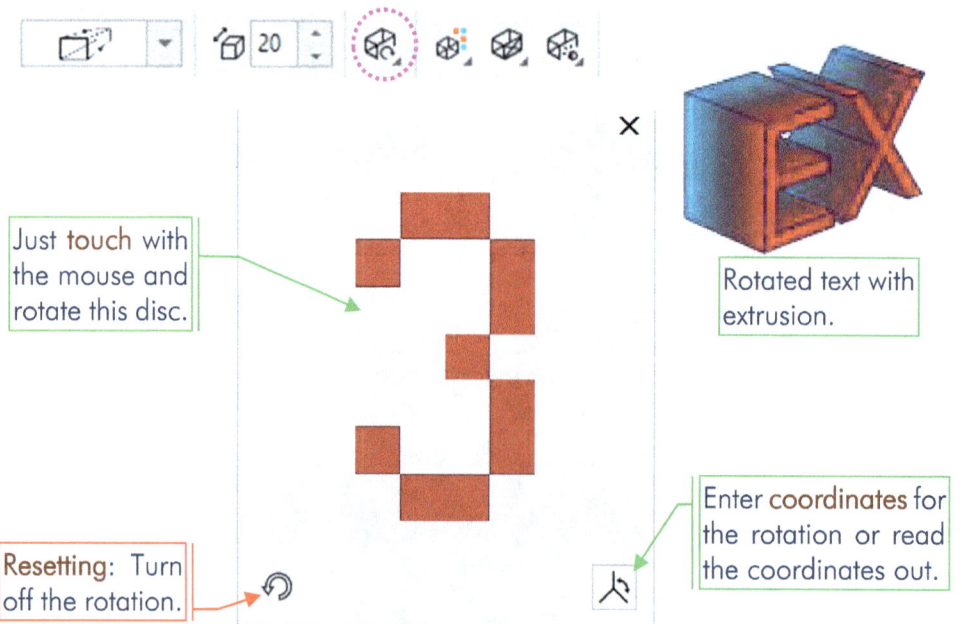

Just touch with the mouse and rotate this disc.

Rotated text with extrusion.

Resetting: Turn off the rotation.

Enter coordinates for the rotation or read the coordinates out.

The rotation often leads to unexpected results, so only rotate slightly, undo if necessary.

23.4 Light and Shadow

For real objects there is always light and shadow. For this, we can place up to three lamps in Corel, which not only illuminate our object, but also create the shadow pages. Each of these lamps can be regulated by their luminosity.

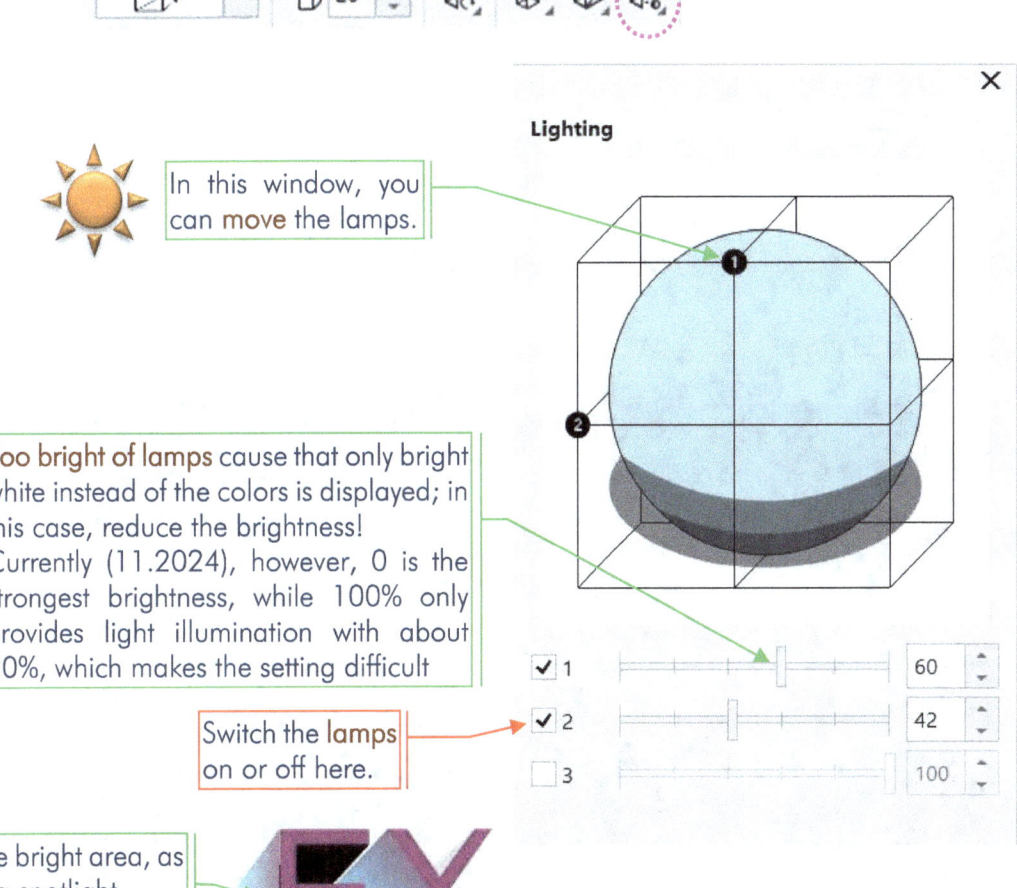

In this window, you can move the lamps.

Too bright of lamps cause that only bright white instead of the colors is displayed; in this case, reduce the brightness! Currently (11.2024), however, 0 is the strongest brightness, while 100% only provides light illumination with about 20%, which makes the setting difficult

Switch the lamps on or off here.

The bright area, as in a spotlight.

Dark shadow sides as in reality.

23.5 Bevels

Here sharp edges can be replaced by beveled surfaces, which is the case with all natural objects, so that the objects become even more realistic.

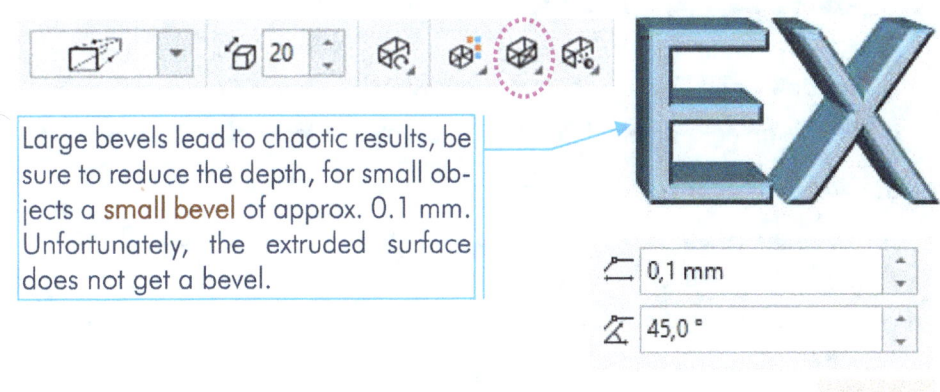

Large bevels lead to chaotic results, be sure to reduce the depth, for small objects a small bevel of approx. 0.1 mm. Unfortunately, the extruded surface does not get a bevel.

23.6 Exclusion Exercise: Extrusion

Try, at last, the following:

- New drawing and first set the paper format matching (how big you want to print out?), then write both text blocks separately.
- Turn them to the same angle and extrude 2021.
- If the extrusion is finished, mark the other text and Object/Clone Effect/-Extrude from, then click on the extruded area.
  - ☞ Thus, the other text has the same extrusion, possibly reducing the depth of the extrusion, since the font is smaller.
- Finally, draw a rectangle as large as the page, with a conical or radial color gradient filling and put it in the background.

Stars with the polygon drawn + Drop Shadow that was offset.

23.7 Summary Shadows

- In the above exercise, we have created a spatial shadow through an extrusion.
- Also, remember that you can create a minimally moved copy as a shadow using Window/Dockers/Transform (s. p. 61).
  - ☞ Assigning a different color to this copy creates a nice shadow.

Shadow Tools not available by Essentials:

- You can create a gradient shadow using the Drop Shadow Tool, described on page 92.
- Of course, the effect contour could also be used to create a soft-running shadow.

24. Finally

24.1 Overviews

24.1.1 Basics

Basics:

⊃ Save cleaned up work in **Folders + Subfolders** and make **backups**!

⊃ Most important programs of CorelDraw Suite:
- **CorelDraw** (cdr): a **vector drawing program** = for presentations, covers, advertisement …, combine photos, graphics and text here.
- **Photo-Paint** (cpt): **pixel** = dots, for photos and photo editing.
- More: **Capture** (make photos from your monitor), **Assets** choose ClipArt or Corel Web Content…

⊃ **Mark** with the selection arrow / **Colors** from the color palette / Set **fills** with the paint bucket symbol / **Rectangles**, ellipses, polygons / **Zoom** / **Group** or combine / Insert **photos** or clip art / **Curve editing** etc.

24.1.2 Shortcuts

Generally:

[F1]	Help
[Ctrl]-z	Undo
[Ctrl]-p	Print
[Ctrl]-x	Cut
[Ctrl]-c	Copy
[Ctrl]-v	Paste

CorelDRAW-Shortcuts:

[Alt]-y	Align on Grid on/off
[Ctrl]-a	Select all
[Ctrl]-g	Group
[Ctrl]-u	Ungroup
[Ctrl]-L	Combine
[Ctrl]-K	Break Combination

[[Shift]-[Page up/down]	Set marked object before/behind
[Ctrl]-t	Text Menu

Zoom:

[F2]	Zoom with mouse
[F3]	Zoom out
[F4]	Zoom on all objects
[F9]	Whole window view (back with [Esc])

Drawing:

[F5]	Freehand pen
[F6]	Rectangle
[F7]	Draw an ellipse or circle
[F8]	Text tool

24.1.3 THE DRAWING FUNCTIONS AT A GLANCE

Here is an overview of Corel's drawing tools. These are located in the toolbox at the left edge:

- **Forming tool** for working with curve points.
- **Pick tool**: mark elements, change size or move.
- **Zoom** to zoom in or out.
- **Cut** the edges of a photo.
- **Pen** (freehand) for painting or drawing, also special pens are hidden here.
- **Paintbrush** and **Artistic Media Tool**
- Draw **rectangles**
- **Circles** or **ellipses**.
- Draw a **polygon**, a spiral, a grid, or a finished shape: arrows, heart, etc.
- **Write text** or insert table.
- Add **dimensions**.
- **Essentials** lack: artistic media, dimensions and connection, some effects.
- Making **connections** (closing figures).
- Here the **effects** (shadow, fade, contour ...) are summarized.
- **Pipette**: Fill fillings and colors from the drawing.
- **Transparency** effects
- **Interactive Fill Tool**: fill options in the Property Bar.
- **Smart Fill Tool**: fast and easy filling with the mouse.
- For all functions with a **small triangle**, additional menus will pop up as soon as you click on them.

Essentials:

(Looks different? Use Window-Workspace-Default (not by Essentials Edition))

Note:

♦ If you place the mouse on a symbol for a short time, the **name** and a brief description of the function are reported. This is very convenient for orientation and searching for a suitable symbol.

♦ A **description** of the currently selected function is displayed in the Learn/Note window on the right side.

♦ If you want to **draw** something, first select the appropriate function (rectangle, line, etc.)!!

♦ If you want to **change** or adjust something, first select the desired object using **Pick Tool**.

  ↳ Beginners often forget to switch to the pick tool and therefore draw many new mini-objects.

  ↳ If you have drawn something inadvertently, undo it immediately, or delete it with the [Delete] key.

> Accidentally drawn miniature objects complicate the selection of other objects and are often only recognizable as errors during printing!

24.2 A Title Sheet

Last exercise, a trifle: A title page for a book.

> ➢ New drawing with book sizes e.g., 23,5x17cm, set grid and guidelines as border lines and
> ➢ write each line of text separately, then align with the left and right guide lines.
> ➢ Then, extrude the first line with short depth, highlight the next line, and clone with Object/Clone Effect/Extrude from the extrusion of the first line (you have to click then on the extruded area). By cloning, changes to the original are automatically transferred to the copies.

> ➢ At the end, draw a rectangle across the whole page to which a color gradient fill is assigned. Finally, place this rectangle backwards.

25. Index

[

[Ctrl] 50
   -Z for undo 34
[Shift] 55

A

Assets 7, 89
Auto Replace 120

B

Background 28, 92
Backup 7
Bars 40
Baseline grid 49
Bevel 139
Bézier 43
Bitmaps 129
Business Card 122

C

CAD 9
Caps 119
cdr 14
Change size 21
Characters 68, 117
Christmas Card 80
Circle 50
   -Arc 103
ClipArt 90
   -File Extensions 14
   -Insert 91, 94, 126
CMYK 69
Color
   -Color palette 35, 72
   -Palettes 74
   -Paper Color 122
   -Pick up 35
   -Scheme 69
Combine 104
Command bars 39
Compressing 10
Connect 89

Copy 23
Corel
   -Fonts 68
   -Overview add-ins 8
   -Photo-paint 130
   -Trace 130
   -Tutor 19
Corner rounding 21
Corner Rounding 143
Corner sizing handles 21
cpt 14
Curve Editing 101–13

D

Default 39
Delete 21, 34
Dimensions 59
Display options 38
Draft 38
Drawing tablet 41
Drawing tools 20, 142
Duplicate 24, 51

E

Edit fill 73
Effects
   -Contour 136
   -Delete 97
   -Envelope 135
   -Extrude 137
   -Letters 134
   -Perspective 134
Ellipses 29
Exercise
   -Bars 40
   -Birthday Invitation 91
   -Blossom 63
   -Book Cover 143
   -Business card dog 122
   -Cartonhome 82
   -Characters 117
   -Christmas Card 80
   -Color pick up 35

-Convertible 42
-Copy 23
-Drawing-basics 21
-Effects 134
-Figures 107
-Flyer 125
-Grafic text 66
-Guidelines 52
-House 51
-Letterhead 67
-Line 41
-Line thickness 32
-Locomotive 83
-Moon 103
-Paragraph Text 127
-Party 101
-Photos inserting 126
-Pick up objects 29
-Pivot point 60
-Pyramid squares 50
-Quadrates 56
-Railway wheel 61, 62
-Rectangle 21
-Rectangles, ellipses 29
-Shadow 115
-Sizing handles 21
-Snake 109
-Symbol font 68
-To the back 36
-Truck 54
-Turn text 66
-Wine 94
Extrude .... *see* Effects

F

File
   -Conversion 14
   -Extension 13
   -New, open, save 19
   -Save 25
Filling 77–89
   -Copy 88
   -Fill types 86, 87
   -Smart fill tool 75
Fit text to path 118
Focoltone 74
Folder 7
   -New, change 25
Forward/to the back 36
Freehand tool 41

G

Grammar Checker 120
Grid 49
Grinding 57
Group 67, 104
   -Features 63
Guidelines 52, 53

-Snap on 54

H

Help 15
Hints 15, 27

I

Import/Export 89
Increase 37
Interactive
   -Filling 96
   -Mesh fill 96
   -Transparency 97

L

Label print 124
Letterhead 67
Line 41
   -Convert in curve 110
   -Line thickness 31
   -Polyline 43, 81
Lineal 59
Lines 42
Lock object 92

M

Mark 29
   -Several objects 104
Mesh fill 96
Mirror 33
move 21
Move 23, 33
MS Office 67

N

Nose 106

O

Overview
   -Copy 23
   -Corel Programs 7
   -CorelDRAW 27
   -Drawing tools 20, 142
   -Sizing handles 21
   -Zoom 37

P

Page 27, 128
   -Set up 28
Page size 28
Page Sorter View 38
Painting 11
Pantone 74
Paper
   -Color 122
   -Color paper 92
   -Size 28

Paragraph Text	121–29
Parallelogram	21
Pen	
-Calligraphic	45
-Pressure sensitive	41
Pencil types	43
Photo	
-Brightness	129
-Cut	126
-Effects	129
-Import	89
-Modify	129
-Scanned	11
-Size ratio	126
Photo-Paint	9, 11, 129
Pick tool	20, 142
Pick up tool	29
Pixel grid	49
Pixel-graphics	10
Planning	8
Poligon	41
Polygon	58
Polyline	81
Position	36
Preconditions	7
Print	124
Printable area	38
Property bar	24
-Many objects	33
-Text	65
-Zoom	37
Property Bar	
-Curve	105
-Interactive filling	96
-Interaktive transp.	97
-Photo	129
-Text	121, 128

Q

Quadrate	55

R

Rectangles	29
Redo	34
Reflect	123
Reshape	81
RGB	69
Rotate	21
Rotation Angle	116
Rounded edges	21

S

Save	25
Scale	59, 123
Scaling	33
Shadow	92
shape tool	105
Shape Tool	80
Size	33
Size change	123
Smart drawing	45
Special Occasions	91
Spell Checker	120
Spiral	57
Square	50
Star	102
Step width	51
Stylesheet	*see* Style
Symbol font	68, 117

T

Text	
-Effects	133–37
-Graphic	115–20
-Paragraph text	121–29
-Text tool	65–68
Text processing	12
Thesaurus	120
Tick Snapping	118
Toolbox	20, 40, 142
Transparency	97, 98
Turn	33
Typographic quotes	120

U

Undo	34
Unit	59
Units	28

V

Vanishing Point	137
Vector graphics	9
Vektor-Pixel comparison	11

W

Welcome screen	19
Wingdings	117
wmf	67
Workspace	8

Z

Zero point	59
Zoom	37, 38

www.ingramcontent.com/pod-product-compliance
Lightning Source LLC
Chambersburg PA
CBHW062216220526
45471CB00009B/3226